INNOVATION

Why a Company's
Toughest Problems
Are Its Greatest Advantage

Adam Richardson

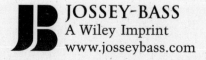

JOSSEY-BASS
A Wiley Imprint
www.josseybass.com

Published by Jossey-Bass
A Wiley Imprint
989 Market Street, San Francisco, CA 94103-1741—www.josseybass.com

Readers should be aware that Internet Web sites offered as citations and/or sources for further information may have changed or disappeared between the time this was written and when it is read.

Jossey-Bass books and products are available through most bookstores. To contact Jossey-Bass directly call our Customer Care Department within the U.S. at 800-956-7739, outside the U.S. at 317-572-3986, or fax 317-572-4002.

Jossey-Bass also publishes its books in a variety of electronic formats. Some content that appears in print may not be available in electronic books.

Library of Congress Cataloging-in-Publication Data

Richardson, Adam.
　　Innovation X : why a company's toughest problems are its greatest advantage / Adam Richardson.
　　　　p. cm.
　　Includes bibliographical references and index.
　　ISBN 978-0-470-48219-3 (cloth)
　　1. Technological innovations—Economic aspects. I. Title.
　　HD45.R45 2010
　　658.4'063—dc22

　　　　　　　　　　　　　　　　　　　　　2009043627

Printed in the United States of America
FIRST EDITION
HB Printing　　　　10 9 8 7 6 5 4 3 2 1

We choose to do these things not because they are easy, but because they are hard.

—John F. Kennedy

Contents

Introduction

A mysterious entity called *dark matter* takes up over half the universe. Though it has been theorized about for decades, until recently no one knew whether it existed at all. Scientists believe it is the glue that holds galaxies together, but we do not know what it is made of, where it comes from, or why it exists. Current astrophysical instruments cannot detect dark matter. The only way to identify its shadowy presence is by observing the influence it exerts on visible matter, such as how it alters the orbits of planets.

In the business world, something equally enigmatic is interfering with our ability to be consistently successful at innovation. Though hard to define, its effects are clear enough: newly released products that fail to achieve the desired goals of growth, competitive advantage, new customers, or revitalized brands, and organizations that struggle to find a focus and identity amid turbulence and ambiguity.

It is a truism now that too many innovations get stalled, squashed, sidetracked, or warped beyond recognition by byzantine organizational processes and decision-making edifices. Some companies have attempted to deal with these internal roadblocks by sequestering specialized innovation teams away in exotically decorated cubicle-free offices, or by ramping up innovation efforts with hothouses (or sandboxes, or kitchens—choose your metaphor). Many employees have been sent to seminars on thinking outside the box with the hope that they will virally infect the rest of the organization.

And yet, one recent study revealed that executives still give odds of worse than a coin-toss as to whether innovations developed with formal processes will have the desired market impact.[1]

Attempts so far to systematize innovation have failed, and innovation processes are often haphazard in structure and frustratingly unpredictable in their success rates. The word itself is so widely overused that it has lost its meaning. Innovation has become an end in itself, rather than the means to create a successful business, improve the lives of our customers, and make the world a better place.

Clearly, innovation is broken. But innovation is not the problem.

The *problem* is the problem.

By this I mean that the scope and complexity of problems that businesses must solve have changed, and we lack the tools not only to diagnose them but also to focus our innovation efforts to be more consistently successful. I call this new breed of innovation challenges *X-problems,* and they arise from the collision of several factors:

- *Disruptive competition and blurring of industry boundaries* as companies leap into each other's spaces, diversifying beyond their core categories into realms previously reserved for partners or adjacent companies.

- *More demanding customers who place a higher premium on the experiential qualities* of using a product—ease of use, how it makes them feel, how it fits into their lives, what it communicates to others—that go above and beyond familiar objective criteria like performance and price.

- *The need to create integrated systems of physical products, software, online experiences, and services* that work as a single whole. Often these integrated systems are the keys to expansion beyond core areas, as well as to meeting customer needs in ways impossible from a more isolated offering.

What I have found from working across multiple industries and geographies is that, remarkably, almost all of them are dealing with this same combination of simultaneous challenges. It seems that everyone was caught off guard. These multifaceted problems are the dark matter of the business world—pervasive, yet hard to see except by their effects: organizational confusion and frustration, and innovation efforts that fail to meet expectations (if they make it to market at all).

While considerable attention has been given to the *internal* reasons why organizations fail at innovation, I believe that *external* factors—the dramatically increased complexity of the problems themselves—are at least as much to blame. If an organization has an optimized innovation process but a poor understanding of the problem, all it is doing is getting the wrong answer to market faster. Up to a point this is actually okay—it turns out that you have to put "wrong" stuff out into the world to understand what "right" is—but obviously no one wants to be doing this on a prolonged basis.

This calls for tools that clarify the problem and help focus innovation efforts more productively. This book aims to provide you with those tools.

The seeds of this book were laid by my work at the global innovation firm frog design, inc. Starting with its founding in 1969, frog design has had a client list that reads like a who's-who of leading-edge companies: Apple, BBC, Disney, GE, HP, Lifescan, Microsoft, Siemens, Sky, Sony, Virgin Mobile, and Yahoo, to name a few. Over the decades, frog has expanded from a traditional design agency doing industrial design and mechanical engineering to a consultancy that does much of its work in the software realm—Web sites, software applications, mobile device interfaces—in addition to physical product design, plus systemic integration of all these elements into single offerings. Chances are very good that you have a frog-designed product in your home or workplace.

The book describes a variety of detailed case studies based on frog's work, in addition to non-frog examples that touch on a range of industry areas. Alongside these "from the trenches" case studies I discuss tools and methods that were developed out of them. Because every company and industry is different, these tools and methods will be more applicable and customizable than is often easily done with highly specific case studies. The book does cover a lot of territory, which is a necessity due to the complex nature of X-problems that involve multiple interrelated challenges. It is impossible for a single book to cover all the issues exhaustively, but a key message of the book is that awareness of the interconnectedness of the issues is at least as important as focusing on any of them individually.

Cross-fertilization of knowledge across disciplines and industries is a core value at frog. What lessons can be taken from work in the wireless communications industry, for example, into the automotive realm? Or for that matter, what about the reverse? To that end, frog is unusual among major consultancies in that it is not divided up by industry verticals—consumer electronics, packaged goods, telecommunications, and the like. This has given me a chance to work across many industries, shifting from looking at the future of toothpaste one day to rethinking mission control for NASA on another.

frog is also unusual for design-centric firms in the breadth of its global footprint, the diversity of nationalities of its staff, and the attention it pays to sharing cultural insights across offices and continents. The company was started in Germany's Black Forest by Hartmut Esslinger, an icon in the industrial design world. Since then it has branched out to eight offices worldwide, which has given me the opportunity to see the perspectives and challenges of companies from many regions.

Beyond the conventional design disciplines, frog has developed deep technical capabilities, allowing it to take software, in particular, all the way through to shipping products. It has also developed a robust strategy capability that identifies new market opportunities, defines business cases, and creates strategies for products and brands, in collaboration with the user researchers, designers, and technologists conceptualizing and designing the offerings themselves.

Much of my time at frog has been as director of product strategy, focusing on these strategic issues and sitting down with executives and product managers whose fundamental question is, "What should we make?" But often they do not even know exactly what the problem is they are trying to solve. They know something has gone wrong, or have an inkling of opportunities ahead, but are unclear how to properly define them, or how to respond. Forty years ago, frog was primarily in the business of aesthetic design—putting an attractive and user-friendly shell around an existing product. Today, the challenges presented by clients are infinitely more abstract, knotty, and high-stakes, getting to the heart of the vision and even existence of their organizations.

Why have companies started to turn to frog for answers to these complex problems? A design firm is maybe not the obvious choice compared to, say, a management consultancy. I see two main reasons. First, it comes from a growing realization that one cannot fully separate strategizing about new offerings from actually conceptualizing and designing them. Our unusual combination of research and strategy with product design and development gives us an ability to not just map possible opportunities but make them tangible with prototypes and shipping products.

Second, frog's consistent focus on understanding end customers' needs, behaviors, and perceptions provides a perspective that complements—and sometimes challenges—the internally generated market, financial, and technical factors that tend to dominate at corporations.

The shift in problem scope from design to strategy that frog has undergone mirrors my own career evolution. I started out as a traditional industrial designer, working at Sun Microsystems in Silicon Valley and creating the look and usability of its high-end server systems. I was fortunate to be involved in early-stage visits with customers to understand their needs for future products, and as the products progressed I helped run tests to see if users could operate the servers easily. This sparked an interest in incorporating the perspectives of end users into the design process. I investigated this further with a multidisciplinary master's degree at the University of Chicago that blended anthropology, sociology, and cultural theory, looking for ways to integrate tools from these disciplines into the design process. Today this approach is quite common and academic programs exist to support it, but in 1995 I was considered unusual.

This experience allowed me to unify design and understanding of user needs. But, like a mountaineer cresting one peak only to discover another, previously hidden, I realized that it was essential to integrate thinking around competitive, market, and product strategy into the process as well. So the last decade of my career has been focused on finding ways to combine tools and approaches that deliver the analysis needed from a business point of view without stifling the creative energies that are so vital to innovation. Today as a creative director at frog I work across the whole breadth of the product development process, and continue to seek ways to integrate inspiration with analysis and vision with pragmatism in order to bring exciting, worthwhile, and valuable innovations to market.

A Quick Fly-Over

In the Prologue, I describe how Hewlett-Packard grew from a simple oscilloscope maker to a $100 billion computer and consumer electronics giant. HP is an extreme case, but the complex issues it has dealt with—moving into new domains, integrating systems, innovating to meet customer needs, and facing unexpected competition—are typical of the problems that many businesses face today.

Chapter One describes the particular challenges of X-problems, and the way conditions in the business environment have contributed to their development.

Chapter Two introduces the Innovation X framework, a set of methods for diagnosing an X-problem and focusing innovation efforts more effectively. The four methods are *immersion, convergence, divergence,* and *adaption,* each of which is described in detail in the next four chapters.

Immersion is about soaking yourself in all the relevant factors of the X-problem: customer needs, yes, but also competitors, companies elsewhere in your ecosystem, issues of brand and organizational legacy and capabilities, understanding of technologies and trends, and so on. Chapter Three discusses ways to research each of these and, more important, connect the dots in unexpected ways to arrive at fresh insights to guide innovation. Immersion serves as the foundation for the other three methods.

Convergence deals with the need to create integrated offerings that meet customer needs in new ways, and allow stronger, more lasting relationships with customers. The term *convergence*, like innovation, is overused. Confusion often arises when convergence is applied to two related but distinct imperatives: *ecosystems* that integrate hardware, software, and services together, and the integration of so-called *touchpoints* that customers have with companies over the course of their relationship, from purchase to usage. Chapter Four lays out a clear structure that distinguishes between these concepts, and allows for precise analysis of opportunities to meet unmet needs for demanding customers and ways to outpace the competition.

Like HP, many companies are expanding into unfamiliar territories as their core businesses falter. In Chapter Five, I discuss ways in which this can happen most effectively with product innovation, using internal capabilities, expanding the reach of what you make, and working with others to deliver systems that are still convergent and address customers' needs.

Chapter Six is about how to use the four Innovation X methods, both before launching a new product and after, to track and adjust to your emerging understanding of a complex problem. Since no one can analyze X-problems sufficiently up front, understanding them is a long-term effort. You also want to track the periphery of your business constantly to spot new opportunities and threats alike.

Complex problems and the Innovation X framework raise some strategic challenges, which I address in Chapter Seven. These range from managing an innovation portfolio to planning product platforms in dynamic environments, and going beyond the common concept of rapid prototyping to what I call *rapid systeming*.

Chapter Eight is about the effects of Innovation X in organizations, as working through complex problems can create challenges in regard to knowledge sharing, collaboration, breaking down silos, focusing priorities, and keeping your organization constantly on the lookout for new opportunities and threats.

Throughout the book I use a variety of real-world examples, some well known and others less so. Some are based on work that I and my colleagues have done with clients at frog design. It is always precarious in a book such as this to use contemporary examples from fast-moving industries, as inevitably they will become somewhat dated and perhaps even quaint sounding. I've tried to select ones that will hold up over time, even if the industries from which they are drawn change significantly in the future.

The focus of the examples is more on consumer products and services than industrial or B2B, and the examples are biased toward technology offerings, largely because it is this area that reveals the cutting edge of the problem complexity that Innovation X is designed to tackle. But the lessons from these should still extrapolate well beyond the bounds of the specific examples.

Definitions

A number of the terms used throughout the book are often cause for confusion. Here are some precise definitions.

Product

I use the word *product* in an encompassing way, instead of making distinctions among physical products, software products, online experiences, and service experiences; they have become so intertwined that—from a *customer's* point of view, which is what is most important—they are the same. For example, TiVo's product consists of a set-top box, a remote control, an on-screen interface, a subscription service, and a Web site. A TiVo customer does not make meaningful distinctions among these elements. I will make the distinctions among the categories, and point out the differences, only where necessary.

Customer

Customer refers generically to people who buy and use products. A customer in this sense may be an individual person or a whole organization. Sometimes people buy for others and are not themselves the product's primary users, for example, purchasing departments in companies, or parents buying for children; in such cases I may specify *consumer, user,* or *end customer.*

Innovation

As noted earlier, the term *innovation* gets used (and abused) in a lot of different ways, so it is useful to put some boundaries around the kinds of innovation discussed in this book.

Geoffrey Moore describes a broad swath of innovation types in his book *Dealing with Darwin* that makes a useful starting point:[2]

- Disruptive innovation
- Application innovation
- Product innovation
- Platform innovation
- Value engineering innovation
- Organic innovation
- Integration innovation
- Line extension innovation
- Enhancement innovation
- Process innovation
- Marketing innovation
- Experiential innovation
- Acquisition innovation

This list combines degrees of innovation (disruptive versus line extension, for example), with business areas (product versus process), sources of innovation (organically developed internally versus acquired from outside), and a number of other innovation categories. The difficulty with this is that they are not mutually exclusive—a product innovation can go along with an acquisition innovation and marketing innovation, for example. This can lead to a lot of talking at cross-purposes.[3]

To this list we could also add innovation efforts in technology R&D (as a precursor to product development for going to market), and sales and distribution innovations. The latter Moore lumps under process

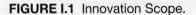

FIGURE I.1 Innovation Scope.

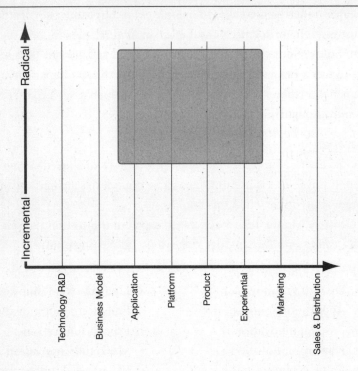

innovation, but they are rich enough in themselves that they deserve their own category.

Bringing these together and doing some synthesizing and sorting, Figure I.1 shows the territory of innovation that is the primary topic here. On the vertical axis is *degree of innovation* from incremental to radical.[4] On the horizontal axis are various *areas of innovation*. These are crudely grouped, but I'm not suggesting a particular order of priority.

The focus here lies broadly in the realm of product development. The upper end of the degree-of-innovation axis is where the most complex and vexing problems occur. To define the areas in a bit more detail:

Application and positioning innovation: Finding a new market for an existing product or technology, or creating a new value proposition aimed at as-yet unconvinced customers.

Platform innovation: A platform establishes an integration layer that simplifies underlying complexity, enabling new products to be built more easily on top of it by third parties. For example, Amazon and Facebook have created platforms by establishing standards that allow other companies to create software that interfaces with their databases, opening up possibilities for innovation that Amazon or Facebook might not have thought about themselves. Today, platforms and products often have to be considered simultaneously as platforms are key to long-term growth in a systemically connected world.

Product innovation: This is the core of creating new offerings and bringing them to market. As noted, I am using the word *product* very broadly to cover physical, software, and service offerings, or combinations of these. The focus is on new-to-world and major line-extensions, rather than incremental improvements to existing products, because the kinds of problems under consideration here cannot be solved by simply improving the products you already have and selling them to existing customers.

Experiential innovation: For Moore, who comes at things from a Silicon Valley tech perspective, this means improving the usage experience rather than changing the utility of the product itself. He sees it as purely relevant to services, not physical or digital products, and as something to pay attention to as a last resort—so-called luxuries like customer service that are layered on top of the base offering. But the line between utility and experience is often fuzzy, and the quality of experiences is not something that can be treated as an afterthought or confined just to narrowly defined services.

Prologue

Hewlett-Packard, the storied Silicon Valley firm founded by William Hewlett and David Packard, started life as a manufacturer of oscilloscopes—lab instruments for measuring electrical signals. If you visit HP's headquarters in Palo Alto you can see a museum of those seminal products, including that very first oscilloscope. In another building you can visit Bill and Dave's offices, located one next to the other, preserved just as they left them after they retired, replete with sixties-era Naugahyde chairs and desk blotters. Venturing a bit further afield, you can also see the garage they rented on Addison Avenue to start their business, which has since been preserved as a historical landmark.

From these humble beginnings in 1939, when Bill and Dave flipped a coin to pick the company name (Packard-Hewlett or Hewlett-Packard?), HP has become a $100 billion computing and consumer electronics giant. It has massively diversified its products, particularly with the turn of the millennium, expanding from its core business of PCs, printers, and "big iron" computers for large companies into such areas as online photo storage, IT integration services, logo design services, and calculators. (What HP does not still make, however, are oscilloscopes; the instruments division was spun off as Agilent in 1999.)

The rapid expansion, set off by profit pressures in its PC and enterprise computing businesses, put HP in a position of fighting wars on numerous fronts against unfamiliar competitors and selling to unfamiliar customers. Many of its competitors were undertaking similar expansions, and suddenly the global map of consumer electronics and computer companies became very complicated. The exhibitor lists at Comdex and CES, the dominant computer and consumer electronics shows, began to look more and more alike. The two historically distinct industries were colliding head-on.

HP's early focus had been on making technical products for use by the engineer or scientist on the next workbench over. That was decidedly no longer the case.

The company has a long legacy of technology innovation—its slogan after all is "Invent." Any of these innovations could be fodder for growth. But given the uncertainties of HP's new direction, which innovations were the right ones to fund and bring to market? That question used to be simple, now it was complicated.

Even as the company expanded, it needed to improve how different groups worked together. Carly Fiorina, the charismatic but controversial CEO who was the first outsider to lead HP and who oversaw much of this period of expansion, recognized the necessity of integration. She wrote in her memoir, *Tough Choices:*

> Everyone at HP, starting with the executive team, had to learn to think about the company as a whole, not just his or her own business. . . . We had to collaborate more because our customers demanded it, and our competitors were beating us; we needed to acknowledge that each division's independence was wasting resources and diluting our force in the marketplace. We had to aim higher and perform better, for it was already quite clear that the company had vast, untapped potential. HP lacked fundamental performance discipline and for years had failed to harness its collective strength and leverage its unique assets.[1]

HP's situation is emblematic of the complex challenges that many companies face today as they struggle to get returns on their innovation investments. It illustrates a variety of factors that commonly cluster together, collectively causing great risk and uncertainty, but (when managed correctly) opening up massive opportunities for growth and giving a company control of the rules of competition in its industry.

These are the key factors:

1. The boundaries of the business are no longer clear. Expansion is happening in multiple new areas simultaneously, leading to uncertainty about where the company is headed, new threats from unexpected quarters, and new competitors. HP's product line expanded from its early focus on scientific instruments into over a dozen different product categories (including personal computers, enterprise servers, digital cameras, and inkjet and laser printers) by 1999. Ten years later the product range had almost doubled again, dropping digital cameras and some other lines but adding diverse new areas such as commercial printing presses, enterprise IT services, and videoconferencing products. HP has consistently sought out new areas to push a core set of technologies and capabilities, giving it a very diverse portfolio.

2. Understanding customer needs is more vital than ever, both to revitalize the low-margin businesses and to understand what new innovations and products will be compelling for customers in the expansion areas. As it enters new markets, HP must understand the competitive landscape and what customers expect from everyone, and which customer needs are going unmet that HP can uniquely address. Straddling the needs of enterprise IT managers, small business owners, and casual users printing their holiday snapshots is an enormous task.

3. Multiple products and services must be integrated together: Customer demand is shifting from individual products to integrated systems of hardware, software, and services. Aligning and integrating these elements (often developed by largely independent groups) is a major challenge. HP has been experimenting with various permutations of digital media in the home—music, photos, TV, and video. For many people, these media and the multiple devices used to enjoy them are too complex and disconnected from one another. HP is trying to address this problem by creating an ecosystem of products that combine to deliver these media in usefully integrated ways for different contexts (living room, office, while mobile).

4. There is no clear right or wrong answer, and the optimal answer will only emerge over time. Indeed there is little agreement on what the problem is, let alone how to tackle it. At the same time, competitors are in a similar situation and the pressure grows to find an answer before they do. Whoever finds it first will reap the rewards (at least, that's the assumption), so slowing down is not an option. HP has been a significant player in the PC category for many years, but as prices have worn down over time it has sought ways to increase margins by tapping unmet needs. Its line of Touchsmart PCs, which feature large flat-panel touchscreens that house all the components of a traditional PC (doing away with the standard box), are one example. At first HP tried out the Touchsmart on consumers as a kitchen computer, with an interface geared toward family communications and storing recipes. It was moderately successful, but Touchsmart really took off with the second generation when HP repositioned it as a living room PC, more oriented toward playing casual games, looking at photos, and listening to music. HP's persistence paid off with a product that sells in smaller numbers but delivers margins many times those of traditional PCs.

Do these four challenges sound familiar? There is good reason if they do. These tough problems are becoming the norm, and HP is far from unique in facing them. Taken together, the four create massive complexity that stands in the way of effective innovation and obscures paths for new opportunities. We need a new approach to innovation that tackles this complexity head-on, and that is what the Innovation X framework was developed to do.

Living in an X-Problem World

This book started from a basic question: With so many companies focusing more intensely than ever on innovation, why are so few seeing the benefits?

According to one estimate, as many as 60 percent of new product development initiatives are canceled before they come to market, and of the 40 percent that do come to market, 40 percent fail to make a profit. In other words, only about a quarter of new product development efforts reap anything close to the desired rewards. Other estimates put the proportion even lower.[1]

Given this track record, some are tempted to give up on the whole enterprise. A rising chorus in the business press declares that innovation has become discredited as a concept and it's time to find the next new trend.

But I strongly believe innovation will be as important as ever. Competition will continue to be based on meaningful differentiation—finding new ways of attracting customers and helping them get what they want done and live their lives the way they wish. Innovation is a key means of developing such differentiation. The trick is how to make it relevant.

Cranking Up the Innovation Engine

Innovation for its own sake isn't enough; it must be focused by clear priorities.

Some years back, I reviewed a lengthy request-for-proposal from a Global 100 corporation. It all boiled down to this: "We've run out of ideas, and we don't know who our customers are anymore." This self-assessment was startling for its frankness, but unfortunately too many companies have let themselves get into the same situation. The focus on cost-cutting, outsourcing, and eking out percentage efficiencies that started in the mid-eighties drew to a close at the turn of the millennium, and companies realized that they needed to reinvest in growing the top line.

Innovation emerged as the primary means to the growth goal. It was the inescapable topic in the press and at conferences, and companies eagerly cranked up their rusty innovation engines and started churning out goods guided by customer-centricity, competitive benchmarking, brand alignment, and market segmentation. But over time, innovation itself became the end rather than a means. We lost sight of the fact that an innovation engine is just a power source. It gets us moving, but it is up to the driver to steer it in the right direction.

Despite this recent intensive focus on innovation, over half of executives recently surveyed by *The Economist* were *still* concerned that they had too few innovation ideas in their pipelines.[2] Not a good sign.

Innovation Surplus

Some companies who have been cranking their innovation engines hard for a few years now have an *innovation surplus.* That is, they have more ideas than they can implement and take to market with available resources. I first ran into this phenomenon a few years ago when doing work with a wireless carrier in Europe, and gradually realized that the benefit of my outside perspective was not so much to help its people come up with new innovations as to filter, prioritize, and refine the ones they already had.

Brian Mathews, VP of Autodesk Labs at the large software company that makes products for architects, engineers, designers, and digital artists, says about his company's own innovation surplus, "The last thing we need is more ideas! The work is in transforming an idea into a form the market can accept."[3]

Even master innovator Google has slowed the pace of new product introductions to refine the ones that it already has. Even if Google could develop them all, the market could not absorb them. Customers are already confused by the huge range of Google's offerings (topping out at around fifty).[4]

To companies in an innovation drought, an innovation surplus may sound like heaven, but it presents its own challenges. Whether you have just a few ideas to invest in or more than you can handle, the challenge is to select the most relevant ideas. As Davila, Epstein, and Shelton write in *Making Innovation Work,* "Too many innovative ideas out there for companies to process clouds their judgment on which ideas are truly great. Clouded by the excess, the companies take on too much innovation and the wrong types of innovation, and waste their investments."[5]

The Goal: Innovation Effectiveness

Innovation effectiveness should be your goal, not just innovation *quantity*. Effectiveness comes from selecting specific innovations to develop based on a clear understanding of what you want to achieve in your business and which opportunities you wish to pursue. Turning out lots of innovative ideas and products without a vision just saps precious resources.

Opportunities for companies come from recognizing and solving problems that no one else has identified. But opportunities themselves are getting harder to spot and more complex to understand and exploit.

Companies must increasingly look for niches, emergent trends, latent customer needs, and narrowing competitive gaps. Profiting from any of these requires expensive and difficult efforts to understand and develop products for them, create the marketing, sales, and support channels, and establish a brand presence. A new opportunity may be at odds with a company's familiar market, with no guarantee that it will expand into mainstream markets and yield the large returns that large enterprises require.

As HP's experience illustrates, companies are increasingly expanding into each other's spaces in unexpected ways, customers are becoming more fickle and demanding, and integrated systems of products and services are superseding stand-alone offerings.

These complex problems cannot be solved by simply improving the products you already have and selling them to existing customers. You need to make a significant—even drastic—shift in what you make, whom you sell it to, the value proposition of the product, or how you help customers with their unmet needs. The question is, how do you figure out which of these, or which combination, is the best one for *you* to pursue?

What's Your Innovation Diagnosis?

How much is the dark matter of complex problems affecting your ability to innovate effectively? Since this is not always easy to perceive clearly, here is a little diagnostic questioning to see which of the typical symptoms apply:

- Can you say what the strategy of your company is in thirty words or fewer? Do you have a clear picture of the boundaries of your business? Can you say what your company stands for today?
- Can you say what central insights are driving innovation efforts and the future of your company?
- Does your organization's innovation portfolio include both long-term big bets and near-term small ones?
- Do you have a deep understanding of your customers and their needs, beyond market statistics and segmentation models? Do you spend much time with customers as they use your products?
- Do you have a clear idea of who your competitors are? Is it a stable set? Do you know which disruptive threats you should be keeping an eye on?
- Can you say what organizational capabilities you have that could be extended into new areas, or meet customers' needs in new ways?
- Are all the ways you interact with customers integrated together to provide the most benefits for you and for them?

If you answered "no" more than a couple of times, then just cranking up your innovation engine is likely to be a wasteful and ineffective exercise, creating lots of noise and heat but not much real movement. You need to get a better handle on the problem itself first.

Wicked Problems

In working with clients from a wide range of industries I began to see the same challenges of complexity, ambiguity, and risk coming up over and over. Some industries had more extreme variations than others, but the issues were not isolated to software, physical products, or services, or to consumer or business or industrial categories. What was universal, however, was that people had a great deal of concern about the challenges but lacked a clear way of talking about them and their implications for business.

After a while, an old concept came to mind: *wicked problems.* This class of problems, involving high levels of ambiguity, complexity, risk, and social discord, was first identified in the 1970s by two professors of urban planning, Horst Rittel and Melvin Webber. Rittel and Webber were struggling with challenges of urban development that brought up complex and interrelated issues of housing versus commercial development, class, economic and ethnic divisions, crime, poverty, transportation, and so on. Each of these is multidimensional and has many constituents with strong views about what makes good or bad solutions, and when brought together for large-scale planning they create a problem of gigantic complexity.

Very little has been written about wicked problems beyond academic journals, with only one recent book-length treatment of them (*Dialogue Mapping,* by Jeff Conklin).[6] There has been a recent uptick in writing on the concept as others have also recognized its value.[7] Nevertheless, if you ask almost anyone today about wicked problems you will get a blank stare.

When I started doing presentations to clients about how they were facing wicked problems, it would click immediately: they recognized the applicability of the concept and were relieved finally to have a name that described their challenges. Wicked problems fall on the upper end of a scale of problem types:

- *Simple problems:* These are problems for which both the problem and solution are easily defined. If you have a leak under your sink, for example, chances are that two different plumbers will diagnose and fix it the same way.
- *Complex problems:* Here the problem is known but the solution is not. For example, the problem might be to design a new product for a price point 10 percent lower than the current model. That's a simple enough problem to state, but there could be dozens of ways to solve it.
- *Wicked problems:* The challenge here is that neither the problem nor the solution is known. How can you define a good solution when you cannot even state what the problem is? That is the conundrum of wicked problems.[8]

Rittel and Webber identified a variety of characteristics that define a wicked problem:

There is no definitive statement of the problem, and each solution reveals new aspects of the problem. The problem is an evolving set of interlocking issues and constraints that change over time and make the problem itself unstable. You cannot properly understand the problem until you have a solution.

Since there is no definitive problem, there is no definitive solution. The problem-solving process ends when you run out of time, money, energy, or some other resource, not when some perfect solution emerges. There is no absolute right or wrong answer. There are better or worse answers, but no way of telling ahead of time what the best approach is.

Each wicked problem is risky because it is unique, and it's hard to test or simulate solutions ahead of time. Some patterns from previous problems can be applied, but there is always a considerable learning curve. One has to place a bet on a solution to find out how it works. As Rittel observes, "One cannot build a freeway to see how it works"—that is, to see whether its impact on traffic and population will be favorable. Conklin notes that this is the Catch-22 of wicked problems: you cannot learn about the problem without solutions, yet every solution is expensive to try and has unintended consequences that are likely to spawn new wicked problems.

There are many stakeholders with different perspectives on the problem and how to resolve it. This makes the problem-solving process fundamentally social. Getting the right answer is not as important as having stakeholders accept whatever solution emerges.[9]

Much of the writing about wicked problems has focused on group facilitation toward consensus on the problem definition and working toward mutually beneficial solutions. Given that wicked problems originated in the public planning and policy realm, this is a natural enough orientation. If you want to solve a problem such as urban crime or plan the route of a new freeway, then emphasizing group perspective sharing and collaboration toward a solution is exactly right.

It should come as no surprise that few people in a business context want to take on wicked problems. Think about it from a middle manager's point of view: how would you like to advance your career by tackling a high-risk, bet-the-farm challenge when no one can agree on what you're trying to accomplish, there's no way to tell when you've succeeded, and the only way to see if you're going in the right direction is to put products out into the market? Not exactly attractive!

But I realized after a time that the definition and characteristics of a wicked problem are not perfectly suited to the challenges that businesses face today—they are both incomplete and overly vague. In the hunt for a better framework I coined the term *X-problems*.

X-Problems

X-problems incorporate all the characteristics of wicked problems but shade them differently, sharpen the focus from the generic wicked problem definition, and add some new elements.

Why call them *X-problems?* The letter X is evocative of many things that apply to these types of problems:

X is extreme: X-problems are extreme in risk and complexity.

X is mysterious: Every X-problem revolves around questions that have never been asked before, or challenges that are unprecedented.

X is a crossroads: A crossroads is a place where things converge together—and diverge outward. At a crossroads one must make a choice among paths, each of which could entail risk or opportunity.

X means opportunity: X marks the spot for treasure—the winnings that come from finding the problem and capitalizing on it before others can.

Several factors differentiate X-problems from wicked problems:

- The presence of competition, and competitors that are getting better and more diverse.
- The need to satisfy more demanding customers and provide superior customer experiences.
- The need to integrate products of diverse types and origins into comprehensive, coherent systems for customers.
- Clarity about the problem emerges slowly, as with wicked problems, but iterative approaches to solving them are necessary, in contrast to the one-shot deal of wicked problems.

The following sections take up each of these in more depth.

More and Better Competition

The major element missing from the traditional definition of wicked problems is competition. This is not surprising, given that wicked problems have their roots in social policy. Certainly, wicked problems address the issue of competition of stakeholders, but primarily stakeholders who have a common interest and will *mutually benefit* from the solution. In a competitive business context, the company that identifies and addresses a problem first stands to gain *at the expense* of the others. In a world where opportunities are getting harder to identify and develop, being first can be very valuable.

(Note that X-problems still may require alignment-building *within* an individual organization, just as wicked problems do. See Chapter Eight for more on these internal issues of X-problems.)

But here we have our dilemma: competition pushes us to move quickly to solve the problem, yet the problem resists rapid definition. Like wicked problems, X-problems cannot be cleanly defined early on because they are too complex and fuzzy. So while every instinct is to decide quickly and act decisively, we must be circumspect, cautious, a little humble about the things we may not know.

Who Are We Competing Against, Anyway?

A recent comparison test in *Car and Driver* magazine pitted Land Rover against two brands that, a few years before, it would not have considered competitors: Acura and BMW. Who at Land Rover, the vaunted maker of continent-crossing off-road vehicles, would have dreamed it would be getting cross-shopped by customers against a Japanese luxury sedan brand and a maker of cars designed for hurtling down Germany's Autobahns?

As described earlier, HP embarked on aggressive expansion over the last ten years, seeking out interlocking areas of business that ideally provide mutual benefits. At times it has expanded the bubble too far and had to pull back (it abandoned its forays into TVs, digital cameras, and rebranded Apple iPods, for example). Nevertheless, the boundaries and focus of HP's business today are hard to sum up in a single sentence. As a result of its expansions, it now fights a multi-front war in many categories against behemoths and niche players alike.

These are but two examples of how once-clear-cut categories of products, customers, and businesses are blurring together. Indeed, the notion of well-defined industries is being antiquated by companies like HP seeking out adjacent areas to grow their markets and satisfy their customers. Gary Hamel argues for the use of the word *domain* rather than industry, as this allows a broader view of a company's wealth-creation possibilities.[10]

A domain is defined by:

- An organizational toolbox of capabilities and know-how, intellectual property, experience, and brand equity.
- A set of products (physical, software, or services) and any ecosystem that surrounds them. Together with the toolbox, these determine the company's place in a value chain.
- Companies that create complementary products.
- Needs to be satisfied for customers (construed broadly).

It is tempting to see your domain as bounded by direct competitors. But as Land Rover discovered, that can result in some surprises. It is better to take a wider view of competitors based on who else has capabilities similar to yours, and who is meeting similar needs for customers, even if they are in a traditionally different market. These companies should be considered potential competitors and your definition of your domain expanded to include them. Yet this opens up opportunities for you; this is much the approach that HP has been taking in expanding its range of offerings.

You also want to be careful of overly defining yourself by customer segments. While these are useful from a marketing point of view once a product is launched, if they always serve as the starting point for new product definition, then you could be limiting yourself. Better to think in terms of customer needs, and see how needs (and their related behaviors and attitudes) may translate to other customer types as well.

Domain shifts set off a domino effect of unexpected competition for others, who in turn must explore new areas. As market boundaries blur, companies are forced to adapt rapidly to turbulent shifts that challenge their core business and their overall mission, as they come up to speed on new domains and learn what being "innovative" means in each them. As Grant McCracken wryly observes, while we might be encouraged to set off for dreamy blue oceans of uncontested markets, the real challenges are the great masses of water coming at *us*.[11]

A company that is highly effective at innovation in one category will carry those skills over when it expands into new categories. If it is coming from a domain with a higher level of innovation, then it will disrupt the established equilibrium. Just ask any one of the hundreds of businesses that never dreamed they would be competing against "search engine" company Google.

You can no longer be comfortable with a circumscribed competitive set. As the question of who you are competing against gets blurrier, so does the question of what business you are in, and therefore exactly what products you should be rushing to market. If you don't know what your target is or who you might ultimately be competing against, should you be moving to market so quickly?

The ability of companies to innovate has become more widespread. Even if you think your company is on the cutting edge, chances are your competitors are closing the gap more rapidly than you may believe.

Steven Jay Gould, the late evolutionary biologist, had a strong interest in how complex systems change over time as different species compete with one another. He was also a rabid baseball fan, and he examined the history of the sport as an analogy to how natural systems evolve and improve. One question he puzzled over was why we don't see batting averages above 0.400 anymore. Through statistical analysis, he ruled out external factors such as rule changes, improvements in equipment, and alterations in league play and season structure. He also ruled out the idea that batters got worse over time (just the opposite—they are better). So what is the cause of the drop in overall batting averages?

He concluded that there has been an overall improvement in play that has narrowed the gap between the very best and the average players. Back in the early days of baseball, the naturally gifted players who could "hit 'em where they ain't" (as Wee Willie Keeler put it while accruing a 0.432 average in 1897) were inherently advantaged over less skilled players. If one were to plot the players on a bell curve, as Gould did, the bell would reflect the fact that there are a small number of very good players, and a larger number of worse ones, shifting the average to the left.

Today that bell curve has shifted dramatically to the right as the overall quality of league players has improved, pushing up against the limits of the human body's mechanical capabilities.

The reason for this, as Gould explained, is illustrated in Figure 1.1. He wrote, "Slowly, by long distillation of experience, players moved toward optimal methods of positioning, fielding, pitching, and batting—and variation inevitably declined." In other words, the gap between the average and the best got smaller, and the gap between the worst and the average also reduced. Everyone got better, and the best are now barely better than the rest.

Gould argued that such a progression over time is a generalized property of complex systems. "I have formulated the argument parochially in the terms and personnel of baseball. But I feel confident that I am describing a general property of systems composed of individual units competing with one another under stable rules and for prizes of victory.... As the system nears [its] narrow pinnacle, variation must decrease—for only the very best can now enter, while their predecessors have slowly, by trial and error, discovered better procedures that now cannot be substantially improved. When someone discovers a truly superior way, everyone else copies and variation diminishes."[12]

FIGURE 1.1 Performance Bell Curve.

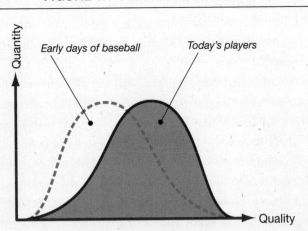

I see much the same situation in business. It used to be that companies that were "naturally gifted" at innovation, like a natural athlete, had a leg up on their competition. They could outmaneuver their competition due to their innate abilities, which came about not through a combination of chromosomes but happenstance of attitudes, skills, choices, and experiences of the founders. In the early days of a new category, this advantage can hold for a limited time.

But the superiority of innovation-gifted companies forces the competition to work harder, to learn better how to compensate for their relative lack of natural abilities. Gradually the overall level of innovative skill in a given market rises, pulled along by the natural talents of some and pushed by the hard work of others. Articles and books are written (I'm doing my bit here to level the playing field), conferences are held, competing products inspected, employees exchanged, best practices exposed, supply chains shared, and knowledge circulated.

Today, not every company is as good at innovation as it wants or needs to be, but the overall level of innovation has risen so that previously lackluster companies have narrowed the gap with naturally innovative companies. It is now harder to stand out and rely on innovation alone as a calling card to customers.

More Demanding Customers

The second difference between wicked problems and X-problems has to do with customers becoming more demanding.

I remember my grandfather shopping for a new car some thirty years ago. He and my grandmother had a farm in Lincolnshire, in the middle of England, and the local Renault dealer had sent a rep out to show him a new model, an exotic feature of which was its electric windows. Magical! No more tedious winding of handles as you paused to chat with a neighbor on a narrow country road or needed to yell at some meandering sheep to get out of the way.

Today, of course, electric windows are standard equipment on even the most inexpensive of models. As cars improved over the years they altered expectations. In turn, cars have been influenced by customers' upward-ratcheting demands about comfort, speed, and capability.

A study of global CEOs conducted by IBM revealed that executives see increasingly demanding customers as one of the top five trends. Customers are more informed, and they are more eager to collaborate with companies on shaping the products that they will buy, use, and live with. But most of these CEOs see this as an opportunity for better engagement rather than a threat to be feared. As one cited in the report stated, "The more informed our customers are and the higher their expectations, the better we will be positioned to demonstrate our differentiation."[13]

These differentiation and expectation trends often translate into increased demand for the aesthetic qualities of using a product, not just its raw functionality. As Daniel Pink has put it, "For businesses, it's no longer enough to create a product that's reasonably priced and adequately functional. It must also be beautiful, unique and meaningful."[14]

Crafting Better Customer Experiences

The term *customer experience* refers to the qualitative experience of using a product: how easy it is to use, the emotions that are evoked by it both during and after use, the self-image that the customers feel they are projecting, and of course how well the product satisfies their needs and desires. The customer experience should be considered holistic, covering all stages from purchasing the product and setting it up to ongoing use and eventually perhaps upgrading, replacing or renewing, or disposal and perhaps recycling. Customer experience is not something that applies only to services or to Web sites; it is a universal consideration.

Customers are increasingly treating ease- and joy-of-use as important purchase criteria, on a par with price and feature lists. In other words, *how* a product does its job is now as important as *what* it does. (Returning to Gould's baseball analysis: over time the capability and price of products in a category normalize, so "soft" factors like customer experience increase in importance.)

Look at how BMW's MINI division has created a big impact with its small cars (Figure 1.2). The MINI customer experience is worlds apart from the typical car-buying and ownership experience. The dealerships are bright and airy, with friendly, helpful, and non-pushy staff. There is a play area for children (complete with models of MINIs, of course). The dealership signage, the brochures, even the Web site and billboards have a consistently designed look, all reinforcing the car's pugnacious personality. Each MINI can be customized to the customer's taste—no preformulated options packages. Once an owner, you feel part of a club, complete with in-person get-togethers and numerous online forums. MINI sells a line of accessories that are not the usual brand-slapped third-party products but are truly in keeping with the brand's "Let's Motor" image: driving shoes and gloves, or a logo-emblazoned handbag that would fit right in at a hip nightclub. This is state-of-the-art customer experience that covers all stages from trying the car out and buying it to owning and living with it.

By taking a holistic view of the experience of using your products, you can often uncover unmet and latent needs that may have slipped through the cracks of a more functionality-oriented perspective. Customer experience is fertile ground for sustained competitive advantage if you can offer clear differentiation that is hard to replicate, attracting

FIGURE 1.2 MINI.

new customers or making the product accessible to previously uninterested people, and building customer loyalty by consistently addressing previously unrealized needs and wants.[15]

In my experience, engineering-focused companies, which are generally staffed by left-brain thinkers who are analytical and quantitative, give short shrift to the softer qualitative aspects of customer experience. But in an X-problem world of heightened competition and customer expectations, this is the kiss of death. Indeed, it is often these companies that find themselves beset by unexpected competitors who woo away their customers by satisfying needs that the engineering-focused organizations had not even recognized. In the 1990s I worked with Oral-B, which prides itself on using rigorous research to design its toothbrushes. It was losing market share to Crest and Colgate, who were up to that point mostly toothpaste brands. Oral-B's brushes were state-of-the-art from cleaning efficacy and materials technology perspectives, but Crest and Colgate were winning over customers by putting more emphasis on fun brush shapes and disposable electric brushes, factors that were not on Oral-B's radar at the time. People had begun expecting more than technical qualities from their toothbrushes—they wanted a touch of joy as they woke up or retired for the night.

Customer Expectations Are Resetting

Companies often focus too narrowly on their own industry and ignore how customers' expectations may be getting reset by seemingly unrelated categories. Customers no longer judge based solely on comparison with direct competitors; they use standards set elsewhere: my satisfaction with a new dishwasher may be blunted by comparison to the ease of use of my iPod, for example. This is not limited to consumer products, either. A recent trend has been for workers in large corporations to use Web 2.0 services intended for consumers and small businesses, such as sites for online collaboration and file sharing. Why? Because the ease of using and setting up these low-end services makes it easier (and more pleasant) to get their jobs done than the industrial-grade systems their companies provide. For all the sophistication of the products from the large software vendors like Oracle and SAP, their offerings are getting judged by end users with the same criteria they'd use for ordering photos online or getting a driving map.

Furthermore, thanks to the Web, customers have an unprecedented ability to see over the horizon of ownership and find out what living with a product will be like. We used to have to rely on our intuition from seeing the product briefly in the store, trusting the salesperson's shtick, or, if we were lucky, reading a magazine review. We relied a lot on tips from friends in the absence of other sources that were unbiased and in-depth. The Web has created a global forum for individuals to rave or complain about products. Anyone can become an industry-shaper. In 1998, Englishman Phil Askey posted a Web page with some thoughts on his recent digital camera purchase; ten years later, this had blossomed into dpreview.com (Digital Photography Review), the premier site for detailed camera reviews. Askey now wields about as much power as anyone in the world to make or break a new camera introduced by a multibillion-dollar corporation like Canon or Sony.

When a company brings out a solid product, this works in its favor. But when it gets it wrong, the reaction can be quick and devastating. The consumer electronics and software categories especially are littered with initially promising but flawed products that were killed off by Web-enabled word of mouth.

The bar for customer expectations is high, maybe higher than you think, and is only getting higher. If you want to bring an innovation to market it has to clear that bar (or find ways to dodge it).

Systems, Not Products

In many businesses, the blurring of boundaries is being accelerated by a shift from shipping stand-alone products to creating holistic experiences for customers. HP's expansion—to cover a broader range of computing and digital entertainment experiences—is an example. The system creates value and benefits in a way that stand-alone products cannot.

For a time the Apple iPod was the product that everyone wanted to emulate. At frog design, we regularly had clients coming to us saying,

"We want the iPod of [fill in the blank for their industry]." But their thinking was often stuck in a product-centric view of the world, focused on the most tangible piece of the system to the exclusion of the vital, but less tangible, other elements. The iPod succeeded by being a systems solution, not a hardware solution, to the problem of digital music. Apple repeated the trick with the iPhone a few years later, creating an integrated system of hardware, software, Web experience, and external application developers that brought high-end smartphones out of a business niche and into the consumer mainstream.

What often goes unrecognized is that *every* product is part of a system. Integrated digital systems such as HP's and Apple's are the obvious examples, but there is another type of system that lives alongside: the diverse set of customer "touchpoints" that include Web, advertising, customer service, collateral, brand, and the product itself. Optimizing how they work together is crucial to superior customer experiences. Companies stand out if they successfully innovate on the quality and seamlessness of these touchpoint systems in ways that address customers' needs, as MINI demonstrates.

It is harder than ever to succeed with a product by itself. Developing complex integrated systems is the new order, and it forces pieces of a company to come together and collaborate in ways that organizational silos had not previously required or even allowed. In the past, the Web team would hardly need to talk with product development teams until the time of product launch, and hardware, software, and service development were often carried out largely independently. Today, these all need to be tightly integrated and developed in parallel.

It also often means that a company must reach out to partners and vendors to collaborate more closely in order to create a system that does not feel to the customer like a bundle of incongruous elements. The IBM CEO study cited earlier also revealed that the top-performing companies collaborate more than their underperforming competitors, working with partners and customers alike to inspire innovation.[16]

X-problems are systemic in nature, and you need an integrated team—both inside your organization and with outside partners—to solve them and to deliver the systemic solutions. Going it alone or thinking too narrowly is unlikely to be successful.

Emergent Clarity

As with wicked problems, the definition of an X-problem emerges slowly over time in waves. Paradoxically, you have' to start making solutions—prototypes, products, campaigns, acquisitions, new channels—in order to further your understanding of the problem. The familiar and comfortable waterfall model of research-analyze-decide-act does not work well here.

Why is this?

It's easiest to explain with a basic example: the introduction of the Sony Walkman in 1979. This represented a truly new product category, and Sony grappled with anticipating how people would want to listen to music while on the move, something they had never been able to do before. Transistor radios had afforded some of the same freedom, but that blue and silver Walkman represented the first time that music could be truly personal. Headphones and cassette tapes meant the songs and the sound were yours alone.

It seems strange now, but early Walkmans included two headphone jacks. Though Sony had the insight about personal music, they felt that the impetus to share would still be strong. Over time they realized that people did not use the device for sharing, and eventually the second jack disappeared. Given the novelty of the Walkman, it would have been hard to accurately test for this behavior ahead of time, and only by putting solutions out on the market was Sony able to home in on the true boundaries of the problem.

Caught between the push of competition to move quickly and the resistive tug of emergence to be more measured, we can think of "time-to-right" as being the countervailing force for time-to-market. Sometimes it is better to have the *right* product out, rather than just the first.

Apple was far from the first manufacturer of mp3 players, the heirs to the Walkman of two decades earlier. In fact it was rather late to the game, and many other manufacturers, from small start-ups to large consumer electronics and computer companies, were pioneering the market. But Apple came out with the *right* thing, the iPod, the thing that cracked the X-problem of digital music by taking a systems approach rather than treating the player as an isolated product.

Apple benefited from not being first. By seeing how the usage model was shaping up based on other players, it was able to use that perspective to its advantage. Unlike Sony, Apple did not have to take as many educated guesses, and could base its understanding of the problem on the issues revealed by the solutions of others.

Managing the tension between time-to-market and time-to-right is one of the keys to dealing successfully with X-problems and matching innovations effectively to business goals.

о   о   о

Like dark matter, X-problems are pervasive but difficult to perceive and understand directly, and are more likely to be spotted by their symptoms. Are unexpected competitors disrupting your business? Are you having a hard time defining the boundaries and focus of your business? Are competitors addressing unmet customer needs you didn't even know about? Are you feeling pressure to fast-track innovation and product development efforts based on very partial information with which to prioritize them? Are you struggling to wrangle internal and external stakeholders so that they deliver a coherent solution? If so, you are facing an X-problem.

The next chapter takes up ways to deal with it.

2

The Innovation X Framework

Armed now with an understanding of the type of problem you are facing, you can explore constructive ways of solving it. I call this the *Innovation X framework,* because it is specifically about how to explore the landscape of an X-problem and then create valuable innovation based on it. As illustrated in Figure 2.1, four methods make up the framework: immersion, convergence, divergence, and adaption.

The four methods can be thought of as bundles of specific research and analytical tools, coupled with principles for how to use them. The Innovation X methods work together to help you understand the X-problem, identify and prioritize innovations, and guide development of marketable solutions based on the innovations. They do this in several ways:

- By creating clarity about the X-problem by dimensionalizing it and giving it as much structure as possible at any given time
- By enabling deep insight into the surrounding context— customers, competitors, brand, retail, organization, and so on—that gives a thorough understanding of possible innovation options
- By showing how your products and their surrounding experiences are meeting—or not meeting—customer needs, and where there are opportunities to meet new needs, expand the ways you can engage customers, and reach new customers that you have never addressed before

FIGURE 2.1 Innovation X
Framework.

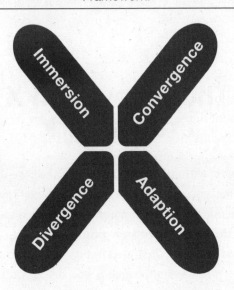

- By describing the boundaries of your business domain, and where it can be strengthened and stretched in new directions
- By creating adaptability as solutions are put out into the world, the X-problem becomes further understood, and new solutions are created and modified
- By providing ongoing tracking of emerging opportunities and threats

Each element is discussed in depth in the following chapters, but it's useful to start with a quick look at how the whole framework fits together.

Immersion

Because opportunities are getting harder to identify, customers more complex in their expectations, and competitors more sophisticated in their offerings, it takes more effort to gain true insights into what the

X-problem is and ultimately how to focus innovation efforts. I call this method *immersion* because it truly requires a good soaking in a broad variety of investigations and inputs that go beyond conventional market research (though that remains an essential tool). Traditional market research often treats customers as data, while real immersion in people's lives uncovers the nuances and unmet needs that inform innovation.

But immersion goes beyond just customer research to provide a full 360-degree view of the X-problem's context. This allows more informed decision making and more effective innovation initiatives. Immersion brings together a multitude of factors:[1]

- Competitors (direct and adjacent)
- Comparative companies and products who can provide useful lessons, but who are not competitors in your own space
- Your company's own business, capabilities, brand, and values
- Broad cultural and economic trends
- Technology enablers available internally and externally

Each of these areas includes a variety of tools, some of which are more qualitative and others more quantitative, whose output gets integrated. Analysis is done *across* all these areas (not just within each) to uncover new insights, find growth opportunities, and detect emergent threats.

Immersion provides the knowledge foundation from which the other methods draw. But that does not mean the other methods wait until immersion is complete, or that immersion halts once the early research phase of an innovation effort or product development process is over. Far from it. Immersion can be intensified for a particular X-problem or project, but it should be done continuously. X-problems don't stand still, so the knowledge gathering and analysis efforts cannot either.

Convergence

Convergence is crucial to addressing the challenge of customers seeking integrated solutions and systems rather than isolated products. The term *convergence* has been in use for some years now, and in fact at frog we made it the backbone of our business back in the 1990s by building up software and Web design capabilities to complement our traditional industrial design and engineering offering. Companies have recognized its importance and have put more effort into creating offerings that converge products, online experiences, and software. Yet confusion is still widespread over what convergence really involves and how to make it work successfully. Do you find yourself puzzling over vague and conflicting definitions of *ecosystems, customer touchpoints, customer journeys,* and *customer experience?* If so, you are not alone.

Convergence, as I use it here in the context of X-problems, means the integration of multiple components (hardware, software, and services), customer interaction points, and enabling technologies to deliver functionality, benefits, and experiences that would be impossible from stand-alone products.

The following model defines exactly what those components are and how to work with them to reach the desired goals, which should help make things clearer. This is important, because without a clear understanding, innovation efforts will be scattershot.

Sometimes these convergent combinations of components are quite straightforward, such as a hardware-focused company branching out into software to extend the range of needs it can satisfy for customers. Other combinations are more complicated, where a range of experiential touchpoints between company and customer are tightly coordinated to bring more coherence and comprehensiveness to customer experiences. The example of the MINI in Chapter One is emblematic of how broad these systems can be, and how effective they are when done well (which is not easy). MINI addressed all touchpoints from researching the car models and how to customize them to purchasing at the dealer and then continuing a relationship with the brand for years afterward.

Companies increasingly need to collaborate with other companies to deliver all the elements of the integrated system. Often, when considering such a collaboration, most of the attention goes toward the value chain (who will make money, and how) and other macro business factors, and much less attention to the resulting converged customer experience, even as customer experience becomes more central to product success. Anyone who has done upgrades to a PC can attest to the frustrations that arise when the new part does not work with the old, and each manufacturer points the finger at the other.

Sometimes this is more subtle than simple incompatibilities. I recall doing research on mp3 players a few years ago and examining one model from Samsung that came bundled with some software from Napster for managing music on the PC (a similar pairing to iPod and iTunes, but from two different companies). The Samsung player was relatively simple and easy to use, while the Napster software was clearly geared toward expert power users. Each element individually was fine, but the combined system came across as schizophrenic because the player and software were at odds in their feature sets and usage experiences.

Just bundling things together does not make for true convergence. The convergence method described here goes beyond how the companies will combine forces fiscally to how the combinations affect the customer, the ease and joy of use, and how the combination provides competitive advantage. Without consideration of these factors, the desired value will never flow through the system, either out toward the customers (by satisfying their needs) or back to the originating companies (as profit).

Divergence

If convergence is about bringing different parts of a business together around a common focus, divergence pulls in the opposite direction and seeks to create a wider view for new opportunities. The growing importance of systems has led to a slippery-slope problem for many companies, who find they must keep diverging and diverging to keep up with the ever-widening system they must deliver and new opportunities that emerge. As the examples of HP and Land Rover showed, this has led to companies cross-competing and moving onto each other's turf in unexpected ways.

X-problems occur most frequently at times of transition and volatility:

- At the beginning of new product categories when everyone is trying to figure out what customers want and what the right recipe is for the products.
- At the stage when a category has reached saturation and is sliding into stagnation. This often sets off a search for new growth areas.
- At the point where a category gets upset by disruptive competitors, causing a rethinking of approaches to the category, and perhaps also a search for new emerging categories.

All three transitional periods have one thing in common. They force changes to a company's domain—its combination of capabilities, approaches, ecosystem, and ways of addressing customer needs. By taking stock of its domain, it can find pathways to new growth, focusing on innovation by building on its existing strengths.

Successful divergence means ensuring that innovations that shift the boundaries of your business still align with opportunities and goals. But you cannot just put new products into new markets and expect them to succeed. Because customers are getting more demanding, products pioneering new territory for a company still must deliver high-quality customer experiences, which makes entering new markets harder.

Adaption

Adaption is a term from biology that refers to the process by which organisms gradually adjust as their environment changes. Here, the changing environment is the emerging X-problem. Adaption is vital for ensuring that innovations match up to opportunities and to business goals.

While the other three Innovation X methods help you build your understanding of your environment and identify opportunities and threats, the adaption method focuses on flexible development of new innovations and feedback loops to course-correct over successive iterations of prototypes and launches.

In the last ten to fifteen years, companies have become much better at making their development systems for hardware and software more flexible, allowing them to accommodate ambiguity in the definitional front end and changes later in the process. The practice known as *agile programming* is a formalized method of managing flexibility in software development. It achieves this by doing away with extensive specifications documents and encouraging rapid release cycles that are put in front of customers early and often. On the hardware side, the Japanese have led the way, building on their flexible production system to make the development processes flexible also.

Flexibility becomes even more difficult to manage with the need to integrate systems of disparate components, each provided by multiple groups, business units, or even different companies. It is useful to find ways to maintain flexibility in these complex systems, while establishing feedback loops on customer needs and business goals.

To sum up, you can think of the four methods like this: immersion develops an understanding of how the world *is;* convergence and divergence conceptualize how the world *could be;* and adaption looks at what the world *is becoming* (that is to say, the ever-changing gap between *is* and our desired *could be*).

All for One, One for All

The Innovation X framework is designed so that all four methods happen largely in parallel. Each method tackles a different aspect of an X-problem and is interdependent with the others. The framework is most effective when the methods can influence each other.

Figure 2.2 gives a simplified schematic view of how the methods relate to one another in terms of intensity of activity over time. For a given innovation initiative or strategic planning exercise, each method will have a period of more intense focus, but each should be in play at all times. (Note that durations of efforts vary so greatly that this should not be treated as "to scale"!)

FIGURE 2.2 Innovation X Methods over Time.

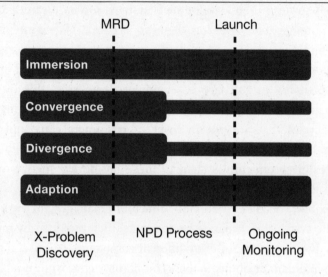

The Innovation X framework is intended to complement an existing new product development (NPD) process and bookend the core product development efforts. By no means does it cover every aspect of conceptualizing, developing, and launching a new product. But Innovation X methods can also be used outside a specific innovation or product development effort, such as to inform higher-level strategic planning.

As Figure 2.2 shows, the four methods are front-end biased to inform the strategic-planning process for new product development. This typically culminates in a working definition of the product's capabilities, customer audience, competitors, and technology and business enablers, often described in a marketing requirements document (MRD). But the methods carry over into the core of the NPD process as the early hypotheses lead to product concepts. In particular, focused, in-depth immersion in customer needs is often needed even after the MRD to refine the product's features and design, since the MRD rarely captures all the relevant questions for designers, engineers, and developers to really sit down and work.

The four methods continue throughout the NPD effort, providing ongoing insight into the X-problem. Immersion acts as the knowledge foundation for the other three methods, but insights that come from adaption, convergence, and divergence should influence how the tools in immersion are selected and used. This ensures that the best insight methods are being deployed based on an emerging understanding of the X-problem. The flow diagram in Figure 2.3 shows how the four methods inform each other.

It is important that the immersion method not be treated simply as an input to the others, because with X-problems research cannot happen entirely before solutions. In other words, do not do immersion first before beginning the other three methods and halt immersion once those other ones are under way.

This iterative process is at the heart of much of the design approach to problem solving, but it breaks with the traditions of strategic planning, which puts implementation *after* formulation.[2] (This contrast may have something to do with why the design process is rising in prominence in business circles.) With Innovation X, formulation and implementation are blended together in a way that is, while not wholly chaotic, less predictable than old-fashioned waterfall decision making. But this is what X-problems require.

FIGURE 2.3 Relationship of the Four Methods.

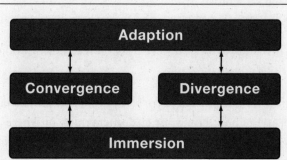

Core Insights

The Innovation X framework will generate huge amounts of information and many options for structuring it. Some of this will be useful at the tactical level for fine-tuning product development. Other outcomes will be more macro in nature and suited for higher-level planning.

Part of the goal in the process should be to develop *core insights,* the fundamental fresh insights that point toward new opportunities and provide the principles for solving the X-problem.

Toyota had a core insight with its first gasoline-electric hybrid car, the Prius. It was that customers would pay more for a car "worse" in many ways than its competitors—performance, comfort, driving enjoyment, cost—if it was turned into a potent symbol for the burgeoning mainstream environmental awareness. This insight guided the development of each generation of Prius, and the way Toyota adjusted the marketing effort around it. Competitors took several years to recognize the same insight, giving Toyota a head start in an important new category.

Core insights are a complement to the notion of core competencies introduced in the 1990s by Gary Hamel and C. K. Prahalad. Core competencies are distinctive know-how that give companies competitive advantage in the market. Hamel and Prahalad defined core competency as having the following attributes:

- It provides customer benefits.
- It is know-how hidden from—and not easily imitated by—competitors.
- It can be leveraged widely to many products and markets.[3]

A core insight provides a different slant on achieving and maintaining competitive advantage:

- *It is logical yet unexpected.* A core insight is the quintessential "Ah-ha," a realization about how your customers think or where a business opening lies that emerges out of combining disparate pieces of data in a way that no one had thought about before. Think about how in a detective story, investigators sift through evidence and connect the dots to reveal the killer at the conclusion. It is always someone unexpected, yet logical in hindsight once the detective explains the chain that led to the revelation. Likewise, Toyota's seemingly counterintuitive realization about what would motivate buyers opened up a larger opportunity for hybrid cars than might have been possible if the company had just focused on straight fuel economy.

• *It provides forward-looking understanding of customer needs and behaviors, and of market trends.* Core insights should not just address the current state of the world, they should provide guidance on how the world will be in the future. This does not necessarily mean that core insights are highly predictive of fads and trends—instead their value lies in durable findings about behaviors, attitudes, culture, society, and business. In recognizing the phenomenon of eco-friendly products becoming status symbols, Toyota was picking up on a pioneering mindset that seemed likely to expand into the mainstream. Core insights are also more likely to provide guidance at a macro level than at the feature level of a product under development.

• *It is "know-why" that is hidden from competitors and hard to guess or reverse-engineer.* Core competencies focus on know-how and can become inwardly focused on what a company can do.[4] Core insights are know-why, outwardly focused on what customers need and want, and they provide the principles that can guide decisions in the absence of detailed data. For example, Toyota brought considerable engineering prowess—its traditional competency—to developing the Prius. But it was the hidden insight about customer perceptions that allowed it to outpace equally well-engineered hybrids from Honda.

It is absolutely vital to have core insights to guide product development along logical but unpredictable paths that are a sustainable match to your current capabilities and future aspirations. As with core competencies, most companies will have just a handful of core insights. A laundry list of insights is a sign that you have not done enough distillation to find the most important and productive ones. Companies that are overly reliant on easily replicated insights become too predictable, making them susceptible not only to their established competitors but also to disruptions from unexpected entrants.

Consider the following list of product launches in the men's razor category:

- Gillette Trac II 2-blade razor, followed by Schick Tracer 2-blade razor
- Gillette Mach 3 3-blade razor, followed by Schick Xtreme3 3-blade razor
- Schick Quattro 4-blade razor

For years, Gillette led the arms race in men's razors, upping the ante regularly with a new generation of products that featured new ways of pivoting the blade head, aloe strips for soothing the skin, and, yes, the increasing number of blades. Schick always lagged one step behind. But suddenly, in 2004, Schick pulled out in front with a four-blade razor called the Quattro. To Gillette this must have seemed like the launch of Sputnik—how could their competitor have achieved this milestone first?

Indeed, the satirical newspaper *The Onion* ran an article purportedly by Gillette's CEO, James M. Kilts, in February 2004, responding to the Quattro. "Fuck everything, we're doing five blades," the fake Kilts says in the article. "Sure, we could go to four blades next, like the competition. That seems like the logical thing to do. After all, three worked out pretty well, and four is the next number after three. So let's play it safe. Let's make a thicker aloe strip and call it the Mach3SuperTurbo. Why innovate when we can follow? Oh, I know why: Because we're a *business*, that's why!"[5]

A year and a half later, Gillette unveils . . . a five-blade razor. With *two* aloe strips.

The real Kilts said about Gillette's new five-blade model, "The Schick [Quattro] launch has nothing to do with this, it's like comparing a Ferrari to a Volkswagen as far as we're concerned."[6]

I think it's safe to say that if a humor publication can accurately predict your product launches eighteen months in advance, you are being too logical and not unexpected enough.

Many of the tools and frameworks discussed throughout this book are geared toward uncovering, recognizing, and acting on core insights in pursuit of solving X-problems. No single type of data is going to crack the problem and make a specific opportunity float to the top—it takes a combination of types of information (quantitative and qualitative user research, competitive analysis, cultural trend insights, and more) to find the core insights that lead to new opportunities. The most useful core insights are derived from a broad swath of activities and analysis that cut across convergence, divergence, immersion, and adaption.

One might think of this as triangulating on the answer from many perspectives. If each effort is happening in isolation, then the value is lost. The benefit comes from the connections and the "black magic" of putting them together, not so much the individual datapoints.

o   o   o

This chapter covers the four interrelated elements of the Innovation X framework, and how it leads to core insights and guidance for innovation efforts. The next four chapters take up each of the elements in more detail and specific tools appropriate for each method, beginning with immersion: how to connect the dots across disparate research data to uncover core insights.

Immersion

You have probably seen one of the successful movies based on the books by Robert Ludlum, starting with *The Bourne Identity*. Jason Bourne is an American secret agent with amnesia, on the run from authorities who believe he has gone out of control. It is a classic David and Goliath scenario: a plucky individual pitted against a massive, powerful organization.

In a recurring trope, Bourne, played by Matt Damon, is charging through a European city, chased by government operatives. The operatives are being guided remotely by supervisors in a control room back in Washington, D.C., equipped with all manner of satellite imagery, digitized city maps, magical remote control of street cameras in another country, and cell phone tracking. Absorbing all this data, the supervisors try to assess the situation on the ground and lead their operatives to the elusive Bourne. What they do not have, however, is a nitty-gritty, real-time understanding of the true context based on ground-level sensory input.

Bourne has no high-tech gear or information from remote sources, yet he is able to act quickly and intuitively. His innovative behavior, if you will, is guided by a long-term goal (to discover his own identity) and informed by an intensive understanding of the unfolding situation, allowing him to stay ahead of his competitors.[1]

The government organization has built up a complex web of data, but its operatives can only see that data as if through a keyhole. By looking at it from a building on another continent with lots of remote sensors they lack the human sensory engagement that is so essential to understanding a rapidly changing situation. Instead of gulping the world in, they must suck it through a straw.

Don't Aggregate to Death

Many businesses still have a detachment similar to that of Jason Bourne's pursuers. Their approaches to gathering customer and competitor information are almost entirely top-down and deductive and lack much bottom-up, inductive assessment. For all the talk of walking in customers' shoes and customer-centricity, companies still too frequently lack a really deep understanding of the daily lives, behaviors, attitudes, perceptions, and unmet needs of the people who buy, use, love, and hate their products. Likewise, analysis of competitors tends to be reduced down to tables of feature lists, price points, and USPs, which strip away the emotional factors that play a large part in customers' decision making.

Businesses tend to have a preference for hard data like that provided by surveys and analyst reports, rather than the soft data that come from open conversations with customers or qualitative assessments of products. As Henry Mintzberg puts it, "The messy world of random noise, gossip, inference, impression, and fact must be reduced to firm data, hardened and aggregated so that they can be supplied regularly in digestible form.... Effective strategists are not people who abstract themselves from the daily detail, but who immerse themselves in it while being able to abstract the strategic messages from it."[2]

Mintzberg notes a number of limitations to the hard-data approach when trying to understand a complex strategic situation:

- Hard information is often limited in scope, without the qualitative richness that adds important context to decision making, such as the expression on a customer's face or the mood in a factory. "A single story from one disgruntled customer may be worth more than . . . reams of market research data," Mintzberg observes, "simply because, while the latter may identify a problem, it is the former that can suggest the solution."

- Much hard information is too aggregated for effective use in strategy making. Especially in large organizations, data sets get aggregated with other data sets, patterns are sought out, and in the process, specific points that may indicate emerging opportunities or challenges frequently get lost.

- Information takes time to harden as it is translated from qualitative into quantitative, or is analyzed and aggregated, so hard information often arrives too late for effective decision making. This is a major handicap in a rapidly changing environment.[3]

Hard data certainly have their place. For example, software company Autodesk has a system of tracking keyboard and mouse inputs for customers who opt in (data are kept anonymous), and this allows it an amazing amount of precision in understanding customer workflows. "I can tell you right now how many people in Japan are pushing the middle mouse button while running one of our products," says CEO Carl Bass.

But Bass cautions that both qualitative and quantitative data have roles. "Don't be dogmatic about your customer research process. There are lots of different tools and they all can have value. The magic, the art about this, is how do you take these multiple viewpoints that are all reflections of the same phenomena, many of which are inconsistent or incongruous, and figure out what to do next? It's hard to put that picture together."[4]

Pay Attention to Your Peripheral Vision

In addition to a preference for hard data, another shortcoming of much business analysis is that it tends to focus on the business that is right in front of the company—the familiar offerings for the regular customers. When I was a designer at Sun Microsystems in the 1990s, we would conduct customer visits to talk about needs for upcoming products, but at that time it was difficult to get permission to talk with customers who were not in the top tier (or better yet, with people who used to be Sun customers but who had switched to competitive products). The result? Sun got very good at designing for its best, most loyal customers, failed to anticipate some significant competitive threats, and saw much of its core workstation business evaporate.

Our conventional business tools are rather like the vision charts that optometrists use, the ones with a giant "E" at the top and progressively smaller rows of letters underneath. The goal is to see how much detail you can resolve in your center cone of vision (only about 7 degrees wide out of 180) by seeing how small a letter you can discern. There are almost no tests for peripheral vision—the vision that lets you see the other 173 degrees.

Peripheral vision has poor detail resolution, but is very sensitive to movement; this is the exact opposite of the central cone, which is great at detail but poor at movement. Peripheral vision evolved for survival reasons—if you were an early human taking an evening stroll, you wanted to know if an animal was coming at you from the reeds off to the side. You didn't need to know what kind of animal it was to take action. But our tests for eyesight ignore peripheral vision, focusing instead on how much small detail you can resolve in your central cone.[5]

Likewise, business analysis often ignores the ill-defined movements at the edges. We tend to focus all our tools and attention on what is right in front of us, things that we can understand in great detail. But it's the unclear movements at the edges that can represent emerging new opportunities—or threats. The periphery is where the disruptive innovations come from, and by the time you can study their existence in detail, it's too late.

Multi-Vector Research

How can you improve your peripheral vision as a business and gain a fuller understanding of an X-problem? You need to immerse yourself in as wide an array of information as you can, and then you need to detect the patterns within it that point to the shape of the X-problem, new opportunities, and possible threats.

You might assume immersion means delving into the lives of end customers so that you can better understand how they use your products, and gain insight into their unmet needs.[6] That is true, but if that is all you consider you are missing out on some important information.

A fuller 360-degree view will allow you to reap the most rewards; I call this *multi-vector research* because it involves researching the X-problem from several directions and then synthesizing those vectors to uncover insights. Figure 3.1 shows a typical set of vectors: customers, competitors, complementers, comparatives, brand, organizational toolbox, technology, retail, and trends.

On the surface there is nothing particularly unusual about any of these vectors. Multi-vector research becomes powerful when you pursue all the vectors at the *same time,* with the *same team,* and with a mixture of qualitative and quantitative tools.

FIGURE 3.1 Multi-Vector Research.

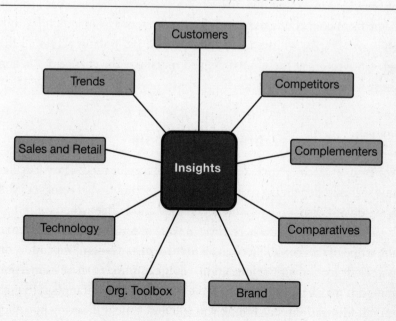

Use a "Multi-Vector" Team to Do the Research

Assemble a multidisciplinary team to do the multi-vector research and the subsequent analysis: engineering, marketing, design, sales, business, and the rest. This means that all the relevant perspectives are included and can be aligned. All the participants should be as familiar as possible with the research from every vector, and they should participate in analysis of vectors that are outside their specialty. This provides as many fresh perspectives as possible (engineers looking at marketing data and vice versa, for example). Do not allow anyone to go off and just investigate their own specialty. Even if the team must be subdivided, pair up people from different disciplines.

Research All Vectors Simultaneously

Looking at all the vectors at the same time greatly increases the speed at which the complexities and interconnected factors of the X-problem can be understood, and affords the team members maximum flexibility for adjusting as their understanding of the problem changes. It also means that a hypothesis that emerges from customer research can immediately be tested out in competitive analysis, for example. The best core insights come from connecting the dots across vectors, not from looking within a vector (that is, within a single data type). By looking across all the relevant vectors at the same time, you maximize the chance of making those unexpected connections.

Immersion Tools

For each research vector, a multitude of tools can be used. The particular mix will vary depending on what you need to know, what resources you have at your disposal, and how much time and budget you have.

The tools discussed here cover a wide spectrum, and it is beyond the scope of this book to look at all of them exhaustively. Depending on your background and organizational context, some of these immersion methods may be quite routine, while others may be unfamiliar, though even if they are familiar I think you will find benefit in seeing how they can be combined, as I describe. (If you seek more depth, please refer to the Bibliography for further reading with the books by Beyer, Buxton, Goodwin, Kuniavsky, Laurel, Rosen, Ulwick, and Zaltman.)

After describing each of the methods here, I give an example of a development effort in which many of the methods were used in combination in order to define the final product.

Customer Immersion Methods

The scope of methods used to understand customers has widened dramatically in the last ten years. "The conventional approach to customer research is breaking now," argues Julie Anixter, co-founder and senior adviser of brand strategy firm Buyology, Inc. "There is more widespread recognition that decision-making is driven by emotions, and happens non-consciously. Companies are moving beyond focus groups and turning to new approaches to understanding the realm of emotion, methods like ethnography, and turning to neuroscience to learn how the people authentically respond to stimuli emotionally. But while those new methods are beginning to deliver, I'm still shocked at how many companies never get around to talking with their customers in novel ways to learn what they care about most."[7]

You need this broad variety of approaches because there are limits to what any given method can discover and make sense of. So a portfolio of customer immersion methods is necessary to ensure the widest sweep, more opportunities for cross-pollination, and validation of findings across methods.

Whom to Talk To

It is important to involve a spectrum of participants in all of the methods. Think through all the people who interact with your products in some way: end users, buyers (who may not use the product), service and call-center personnel, sales staff, influencers on purchase choices, workers who assemble the product or disassemble it for recycling, and so on.

For X-problems in particular, it can often be helpful to focus on lead users and adjacent customers. Lead users are people who use your product in extreme ways. They are not typical, and there's always the possibility that they are just outliers, but their behaviors can often presage more mainstream usage in the future. Adjacent customers are people who use products in adjacent categories, or who have needs that overlap with what your products do, but choose other solutions. Talking with them can point in new directions of opportunity.[8]

Ethnography

Ethnographic techniques have become more common in the last few years. They involve spending time with customers as they do relevant activities that involve your product, but also activities that surround it contextually. These are often done in the environment where the product is used and never isolated in a focus group room, so there is the additional opportunity to pick up ambient information about the people, such as their hobbies, how a family shares information (look at the fridge, or the notes board in the kitchen), whether products are bought individually or in sets (look at their kitchen knives or stereo equipment, for example), or whether comfort levels with technology are uniform across product categories. These clues can lead to larger insights and open avenues for discussion of attitudes and behaviors that may affect your product.

Ethnographic visits are typically done by teams of two or three researchers (more than that and you overwhelm the participant). One researcher (typically the lead, who stays constant across all the visits) is totally focused on the dialogue with the participant, actively listening and steering the conversation. An assistant takes notes, operates the photography or video gear, and provides a second interpretive ear. Staff from *all* disciplines should attend some ethnographic visits, at least as observers, so that everyone gets firsthand experience of customers' lives and needs.

In the course of a project at frog to design kitchen appliances for a company called Turbochef, which makes ovens that cook food more than ten times faster than a normal oven, we visited many people in their homes. We talked about how they cooked, why they enjoyed cooking or found it a chore, and how food and cooking fit into their family life and routine. Amid the philosophical questions, we also addressed more granular issues of ease-of-use, purchase criteria, brand, and aesthetics.

Several people reminisced about the old Wedgwood stoves in their grandmothers' kitchens, and had fond memories of their white porcelain finishes and welcoming rounded shapes. They were tiring of the stainless steel industrial look popularized by the dominant high-end brands, Viking and Wolf. The modern ovens would poke you in the back if you leaned up against them, complained one woman, but the Wedgwoods were soft and inviting. The old ovens encouraged people to gather in the kitchen, which in recent years has become where entertaining is done (not just prepared for), and where parents can keep an eye on kids playing or doing homework. So we designed handles on the Turbochef appliances that were smooth and blended in to make them more comfortable to crowd against. This detail, together with many other insights, led to appliances that looked different and worked dramatically differently from anything on the market.

Journals

Ethnography provides a snapshot of someone's life, but often we need a more long-term understanding of their behaviors. Having participants fill out journals for a week or more that capture their day-to-day (even hour-by-hour) activities, feelings, and wishes can provide that longitudinal view. Journals are increasingly Web-based today, making use of camera-phones, but can also be done with plain old pen and paper.

Surveys and Focus Groups

Traditional surveys and focus groups have their place, but early in understanding an X-problem, both should be treated with extreme caution. These formats are too narrow for the very open-ended discovery that must occur at the beginning of X-problem research. They tend to force too many premature assumptions about the problem that may obscure the real insights. Later, as the hypotheses, concepts, and insights into trends and needs firm up, the more quantitative findings from these methods are much more valuable. After product launch, they can also provide a perspective on the gap between what customers want and what the product is delivering, and on changes in customer needs and macro trends.

Customer Collaboration

Forward-thinking are striking up more two-way collaborative relationships with their customers, by asking them to participate in shaping new product concepts, not just passively react to them. Web sites like MyStarbucksIdea and Ideastorm, operated by Starbucks and Dell respectively, provide open forums for customers to offer suggestions in various categories. While there is a lot of repetition, and some of the ideas are just unfeasible, genuine nuggets also appear, and companies get a real-time, almost free, gauge of trends.

Customers are more informed, and more eager to collaborate with companies on shaping the products that they will buy, use, and live with. Progressive companies see this as an opportunity for better engagement rather than a threat to be feared.[9] As a product moves through development, keep customers involved. Do not wait to include them just for last-minute-too-late-to-do-anything-with-feedback testing—engage them early and often.

One of the ways we do this at frog design is with Participatory Design Sessions. In PDSs we invite customers to try out concepts still at the early model or drawing phase, and have them move pieces around or construct their own idealized products out of kits of parts (from which they are free to configure things however they want, and invent features we have not thought of). We may ask them to show us how they use the product so that we have a sense of context and do not just take the feature at face value.

A benefit of this is that product concepts are pushed very early in the process, while we are still deep in immersion and trying to formulate our understanding of the X-problem. This may seem like a radical or perhaps even cart-before-the-horse approach, but getting half-baked prototypes in front of customers as quickly and frequently as possible pays big dividends:[10]

- Early concepts ("solutions") uncover new perspectives on the X-problem that would not have appeared if we had stayed purely in research mode. Solutions beget a fuller understanding of the problem.

- Concepts help make the future possibilities more concrete, and make the X-problem more tangible. Combined with rich findings from customer visits and all the other immersion vectors, this gets people excited and motivated in a way that a more sterile marketing requirements document may not.

Usability Testing

Testing for ease of use has become common practice as companies recognize that customers will use the product in unexpected ways, and that assumptions by the development team about product usage may be incorrect. Usability testing allows controlled and instrumented evaluation of designs to see how long tasks take to complete, what comprehension problems customers have with a product, and what specific elements they like or dislike.

Still, a common mistake is to leave usability testing until late in the process, where changes are hard to do, expensive, or both. The cost and difficulty of making changes goes up exponentially as the ship-date approaches, but a more incremental method of usability testing that starts earlier will catch the major issues sooner. Early on, the dividing line between PDSs and usability testing is blurry, but as the product gets more refined, there are benefits from the more controlled procedures of usability testing.

Competitive Immersion Methods

Because of the challenge of unexpected competitive entries (which often spark an X-problem) and blurring of industry boundaries, you need to take a liberal view of who your competitors are. Analyzing competitors with an industry-specific focus will be too limiting. Instead, take a broader, more domain-based view by asking yourself questions like these:

- What other companies have similar toolboxes of capabilities and know-how that could diverge into your area? (Acura and BMW, for example, had much the same capabilities as Land Rover; what kept them traditionally separated was just a matter of positioning.)

- Could a company lower down in the supply or value chain work its way up, possibly with a low-cost play? Are there companies elsewhere in the supply or value chains that you could displace? (For example, the launch of private label brands from Office Depot and Best Buy has put them in competition with companies that they previously were just retailers for. Toyota's Scion brand of highly customizable cars has captured revenue that used to go to a ragtag array of third-party modification firms and parts suppliers.)
- What other companies are addressing the same or similar needs to your own products, even if they are not strictly in the same category? (Cameras in cell phones have significantly affected sales of low-end digital cameras, for instance.)

Go beyond stats and figures for both direct and potential competitors and get to some of the more subtle qualities that may allow a competitor to succeed or fail. Often these revolve around issues of customer experience, product and brand perception, and ecosystem integration. Technically superior products with longer feature lists do not always win out against similarly priced but traditionally inferior products, and the reasons why may be quite different from the measures on which you normally compete and define the category.

To understand the nuances, do not just analyze competitive products by looking at Web sites (unless the company is Web-based) and by handling them in stores. Buy them, use them in ways that end customers will (who may have quite different needs and motivations from you), sign up for services for months at a time, and gain a full understanding of the end-to-end experience. Subtle reasons for competitors' success may not show up in spec sheets, but can become clear through longer-term exposure.

During the development of the second-generation Taurus in the late 1980s, Ford management took turns driving a Toyota Camry around. This led them to pay extra attention to the drivetrain and fit-and-finish on the interior. Mary Walton writes in *Car,* her exhaustive history of the development of the second Taurus, "Camry engineers had gone to extraordinary pains in the design of every component. Moreover, some parts were identical to those in the Lexus. That kind of quality didn't come cheap. Toyota had spent maybe $1,000 per car more than the amount budgeted for the Taurus."[11]

The Taurus team's goal then changed from a convoluted corporate-speak mission statement to something supremely simple: "Beat Camry."

On the other hand, many automakers provide cars to their high-level employees on a regular basis, which ensures that those people always have new vehicles. They never have to deal with oil changes, dead batteries, and the normal issues that come up with older cars, so they get a skewed perspective on their own products.[12]

You should also be evaluating your own products in the same way as you do competitors', and using them for the same prolonged periods. "Eating your own dog food" is a colorful software development expression for using the product that you are developing. This deceptively simple step can reap great rewards, and if you skip it you risk missing opportunities to fix problems.

A number of years ago, I was part of a team conducting research with a U.S. wireless carrier whose leadership wanted to find out how to improve their products and relationships with their customers. When we interviewed company executives, we found that they did not use the company's own products; they used BlackBerrys, which at the time were not sold by this carrier. So the executives did not have good firsthand knowledge of how their products or service performed. Not using one's own products can lead to a lack of empathy with customers, with the result that their priorities do not drive your priorities or innovations.

Complementers Immersion Methods

Complementers are products that provide complementary functionality to your own, and are used alongside. They are not integral to the functionality of your products, so they are not necessary for your product to work. However, they satisfy needs that your products do not. For example, a table is a complementer to a chair—the chair works fine without the table, and other things can be substituted for the table to provide a horizontal surface, such as a desk. Accessories like cases for electronic gadgets are typically complementers. A downloadable game for a cell phone would be a complementary product, while a game for a video game console would not, since it is integral to the functionality. (I return to these distinctions in Chapter Four.)

Complementers should be examined with much the same questions and hands-on usage as competitors:

- What toolboxes of capabilities do companies making the complementary products have? Could they be at risk for expanding into your direct area, becoming competitors? Could they move to a position in the value chain that could be a threat to yours?
- Are the complementary products addressing similar needs to your products? Could they be adapted to do so? Are there needs the complementers are satisfying that your products could be adapted to?
- Are there products from seemingly unrelated categories that are being, or could be, used to fulfill the same needs for customers as your products?

Comparatives Immersion Methods

Comparatives are not direct competitors but are analogous examples that provide lessons relevant to the X-problem. Comparative immersion, combined with competitor and complementer immersion, can be a powerful tool for shedding new light on problems and giving a new perspective that may open fresh avenues for differentiation. What could an airline looking to improve its customer service, for example, learn from service superstars like online shoe store Zappos or outdoor equipment retailer REI?

For one project at frog that had to do with hard drives, we hired a home organization consultant, someone who gets hired to help people declutter their houses. We thought we might be able to take some lessons from how people approach organization in the physical world and apply it to the organization of digital data. She gave insight, for example, into how people categorize stuff based on the need for immediate access. This made us realize that hard drives are often treated like the big plastic boxes we all have in our garages, basements, and attics where *stuff* is tossed, out of sight and out of mind. On a hard drive, all our stuff is also treated basically the same, even though some of it needs to be accessed very frequently, while other things can go into deep storage. This led us to think about how the drive itself could facilitate better organization, beyond what the computer's operating system already did.

Organizational Immersion Methods

This looks inward at the company itself: its values, its goals and strategies, metrics for success (both explicit and implicit), and tolerance for risk and change, its product lines and capabilities, past efforts at solving similar kinds of problems, and the technologies, IP, and product concepts that are available for use.

These items make up the *toolbox* of the organization, which I discuss in more detail in Chapter Five. Each of these organizational factors holds promise for being extended, built up, and used in new ways.

Companies that have a strong sense of self-identity, and have well-understood principles guiding their growth that give boundaries along with flexibility, tend to do better when facing X-problems. It is also important to understand how collaboration happens across the organization, its capacity for working with outside partners, its tolerance for radical new ideas, and how decisions are made and communicated.

Brand Immersion Methods

Whereas organizational immersion is inward-focused, brand immersion is outward-focused: what is the persona you wish to convey to customers, and how do they actually perceive you?

Is your brand clearly defined and widely understood within your organization? For many companies it is not. Or it may be well defined but only really well understood by a small number of people in the executive suite or marketing. Bruce Temkin, VP at Forrester and author of the "Experience Matters" blog, observes, "Companies generally do an inferior job of using their brand as an input to the design and development process. If you don't have a strong view of your brand then you don't have the guide-posts that allow you to make decisions consistently about how to deliver for customers."[13]

In terms of addressing a particular X-problem, it is often helpful for the team working on it to get together and consciously align on their understanding of the brand. This will help the team make choices about what kinds of innovations are most appropriate to pursue, as the brand provides principles about what the company does—and does not—do.

Ideally you will have ongoing brand-tracking studies that answer the question of how customers perceive you. These can be achieved through surveys, focus groups, informal conversations with salespeople, and scanning of online forums and blogs.

Trends Immersion Methods

Large-scale social and cultural trends can often seem too abstract and ethereal to be meaningful to tactical product development. In fact, however, trends can have unexpected impacts.

In the 1980s, Xerox changed the colors of the handles on its copiers to purple. Why? It had nothing to do with color trends. Instead, multiple large-scale shifts joined forces to decimate Xerox's traditional copier business. The world of commerce was speeding up, thanks to FedEx and faxes. Business staff had to be more self-reliant, thanks to the elimination of secretaries, which meant that copiers had to be easier to use without training, and couldn't require waiting for a mechanic to fix them. Canon and other competitors were encroaching on Xerox's business from the low end with inexpensive, easy-to-use and easy-to-service machines that fit this confluence of forces perfectly.

All this led Xerox to radically overhaul its business model away from its reliance on service contracts. At the same time it overhauled the design of its machines inside and out to improve ease of use for untrained workers, one element of which was the consistent use of purple handles on the outside to designate access points for paper and toner.

Gaining insight into current and emerging trends is an exercise in multi-vector research. Tap knowledge from subject matter experts who are not your customers. They can help a team grappling with an unfamiliar domain quickly come up to speed. And they can provide insight into customers' behaviors and trends, or perspectives from outside your domain that are analogous.

Lead users—the customers who push the boundaries of how your products are used—can be indicators of trends on the upswing. Standard methods like analyst reports, scans of Web sites, blogs, forums and magazines, and review of internal customer feedback from sales channels can all be valuable inputs about emerging trends. Across this broad swath, you are looking for the small signals that indicate a pattern starting to emerge.

For a project at frog a few years ago designing televisions, we identified a trend that we dubbed "The Bad Boy Wears Prada." This trend was about how it was becoming more acceptable for men to be attentive to interior decor, retaining their masculinity at the same time. Several signals pointed in this direction:

- So-called "man caves" were becoming a popular add-on for new housing developments as well as re-models. These were "men-only" areas of a home where guys could hang out with their male friends, watch sports on a big-screen TV, and relax in recliners. They were often lavishly decorated and expensively appointed with home theater systems, wood paneling, full bars, dartboards, and framed movie and sports posters. Man caves had become the most popular upgrade for new home purchases in the Dallas, Texas, area, adding up to $15,000 to the home price.
- Several TV shows were putting forward models of men caring about their appearance and manners (*Queer Eye for the Straight Guy*) and fashion (*Two and a Half Men*) without seeming effeminate.
- Magazines such as *Cargo* and *Maxim* blended *Playboy* with shopping, making it OK to ogle scantily clad women alongside Bruno Magli shoes.

This led us to think about how the aesthetics of the television needed to fulfill differing needs for both sexes, and how the television may be used quite differently by women and men.

If you need to get in touch with the avant-garde of culture to inform product aesthetics or message, an interesting and enjoyable technique is the *inspiration tour*. This involves visiting locations that represent the cutting edge in cities like New York or Seoul, to soak in the sights, sounds, colors, clothes, stores, and of course, people. Not just random strolling around, inspiration tours are best achieved with careful planning ahead to maximize the value of the time on the ground. Draw on local experts and knowledge to map out specific stores, venues, and cultural hotspots to visit, line up talks with local culture mavens and influencers, even spend an afternoon with people who are leading edge or mainstream and do some informal ethnography.

Sales and Retail Immersion Methods

Understanding the purchase process is often a critical piece of the puzzle, particularly when trying to shift customers' perceptions from a familiar, mature category with a disruptive product. How do people evaluate product options? How do they research choices, if at all? What impacts do the retail setting and staff have?

Spending time observing, and if possible questioning, customers in the retail environment can be invaluable. Techniques include pretending to be a customer, shadowing real customers and asking them about their decision-making process as they live it, intercepting customers as they ponder choices at the shelf, interviewing sales staff, attending sales staff training sessions, and talking with store buyers. If you sell directly or through other channels than retail, in-person interviews and watching as buyers go through the purchase process is equally important. What roadblocks do they hit? How is the process supporting their needs and anticipating their questions or concerns? What are the processes for resolving them effectively?

Technology Immersion Methods

Technologies enable new product capabilities and customer experiences, and also place constraints on them. Gaining a thorough understanding of these as early as possible is vital. What are the current and emerging technologies relevant to the domain and the X-problem? Are there technologies not traditionally used in this domain that could be applied? If you are diverging into a new domain, do you bring some technologies that others do not have? Do competitors in a prospective domain possess technologies that you will need to acquire?

Immersion Synthesis

Before moving on to look at the rest of the Innovation X methods, it's useful to pause to get a better picture of how analyzing multi-vector research comes together to inform convergence, divergence, adaption, and, ultimately, product strategy. This is a process called *synthesis,* a term used to distinguish it from analysis, since it requires an active and creative blending and filtering of the data.

Describing a simple how-to process for synthesizing the rich data coming out of a multi-vector immersion is difficult because the process changes considerably based on the context of the problem. Each synthesis differs from all the rest.

The amount of information that can come out of multi-vector research is staggering. I recall staring at a wall of data during one analysis session, four hundred discrete points all written out on Post-it notes. Absorbing that much information is like driving the old MG convertible my wife used to have—viscerally overwhelming, thrilling, but a bit scary.

Making sense of huge quantities of heterogeneous information with a collaborative, multidisciplinary team is much easier when you can spread all the information out and literally, not just metaphorically, immerse yourself in it.

A first step is to get out of the virtual realm: the computer screen is like the keyhole Jason Bourne's pursuers were looking through. It is limiting and gets in the way. Being physically immersed in the information makes it far easier to concentrate on the data points themselves: all the customer research observations, quotes and photos, samples of competitive products, and printouts of Web pages and

PowerPoint slides. One can more easily get into a state of flow in which thoughts stream in and build on one another without distractions like e-mail and calls.[14]

If information is on paper it can easily be moved around, combined with other pieces of information, seen by many people at once, spied in one's peripheral vision, highlighted and annotated, or duplicated. I remember one client doing research analysis by passing around a Word document between team members. Within the document were electronic "Post-its" where each person typed in research findings. This is not the same thing at all! At frog we go through Post-it notes at an enormous rate. They are stuck to $4' \times 8'$ pieces of black Foamcore so they are portable and easy to rearrange. Exploding the data out makes it simple to add new data as they arrive and to reconfigure the data points in clusters and patterns as the shape of the problem emerges and gets refined.

It also maximizes the opportunity for making happenstance connections that can lead to fresh insights. Rather than having to dig through PowerPoint slides, spreadsheets, or some file on who-knows-which computer, we can take advantage of our brains' amazing ability to remember physical locations and relationships, and the muscle memories that our bodies retain. "Where did I see that? Yes, it was over on this side of the room on a pink sticky...." Ten seconds later you've found that piece of information that you put up two weeks ago.

Zoom, Zoom

Another benefit of the physical display of all the research is that it helps details stay present, but within the broader context. With X-problems the idea is to seek out the small signals that will open new opportunities or reveal emergent challenges. Remember that you are expanding your peripheral vision here, so subtle things can be important. It is vital not to allow details to get lost and rounded over in the drive to aggregate the information.

A client who was involved in a multi-vector process with us at frog once remarked, "You never throw anything away; nothing gets left behind." Too many companies have research processes that are one-way aggregation pipelines—a continual zooming out of perspective and with it a reduction of detail. This is deadly when dealing with X-problems. You have to be able to zoom in and out in detail level and constantly make connections between small and big things.

Again this goes back to maximizing the opportunity for happenstance connections that can lead to fresh insights. As we move through the research process and improve our understanding of an X-problem at frog, we will plow through a lot of data. What may seem irrelevant early in the process can suddenly become highly relevant later as our understanding improves. We want to make sure we have not prematurely thrown out a piece of information. Making it physical and visual improves our chances of remembering it, finding it, and connecting with it again.

○   ○   ○

To give a taste of how the vectors can come together and reinforce one another, the case study below presents an example of a client with whom frog design worked on a thorough immersion process.

Immersion Case Study: IPC

Unless you are a stock trader, it is unlikely that you have heard of IPC. In fact, many stock traders aren't that familiar with IPC either, even though they probably have one of the company's devices sitting on their crowded desks on the trading floor. And that was part of IPC's challenge—despite strong brand awareness with IT buyers at trading firms, awareness with traders themselves was quite low, and many took its products for granted. Despite IPC's dominance in the category, traders often overlooked the pivotal role that its products play in helping manage the chaos that plays out every day in a stock exchange.

IPC makes what are known as "turrets": highly sophisticated, multi-thousand-dollar units for handling hundreds of incoming and outgoing phone calls, each of which is urgent and mission-critical. It's a sophisticated phone with the stout build of a linebacker, helping the trader stay on top of the chaos in a rough-and-tumble environment.

IPC's previous generation turret was about twelve inches wide in its basic configuration, and two long, skinny LCD screens ran across its black surface. Dozens of buttons above and below each screen controlled the calls, and the function of each button changed depending on what was on the screen next to it. There was a speakerphone at one end for intercom calls, a unit for handling group calls and what are known as "hoots" — large group calls used for analyst briefings as well as actual trades. It looked rather like a shrunk-down airplane cockpit.

IPC recognized that a new generation of turret was needed to meet the changing needs and expectations of traders. "The trading floor is one of the most high-octane and high stakes environments in business," observes Lance Boxer, CEO of IPC. "With the advent of cell phones, iPods and Xboxes, the new generation of traders has been weaned on consumer technology. This has had a profound influence on expectations of tools in the workplace."[15] People sometimes assume that the need for customer experiences only applies to consumer products, but IPC recognized its importance in its highly charged, utility-driven environment. By improving traders' work effectiveness it would raise IPC's awareness.

"A trader is only as good as his or her tools, and we realized that with the proper research, we could profoundly change the trader experience," says Boxer. "We wanted to achieve a more integrated relationship with everything that is going on in the trading environment and to give traders a more modern and innovative tool that would enhance job performance."[16]

A team in frog's New York studio collaborated with IPC on creating the new turret. Since no one at frog was a professional stock trader, the first thing the team had to do was understand the day-to-day life of traders on a busy trading floor. They visited numerous financial and securities firms, as well as the New York Stock Exchange floor, to observe the working conditions. There they found that traders dealt with a multitude of devices and monitors in a cramped workspace, developing many ad hoc workarounds to use the equipment in preferred ways. Former investment bankers in the frog office provided additional perspective on the field observations, and the team also had access to ongoing global research that IPC was already conducting.

The team embarked on a wide-ranging immersion that used many of the tools I have just reviewed. IPC had a number of known challenges going into the development, and in its multi-vector research the team uncovered a few additional ones. By connecting findings across vectors, new insights and design approaches were uncovered that dramatically improved the product and led to strong adoption and demand from end users. Figure 3.2 shows the end result: the IQ/MAX turret.

FIGURE 3.2 IPC IQ/MAX Turret.

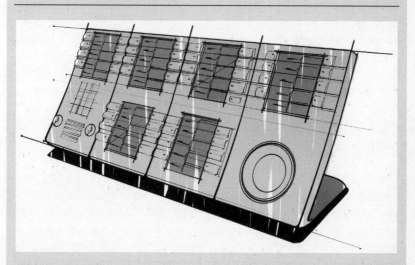

Challenge: Keep IPC competitive in the face of new, less expensive entrants

Competition Vector: IPC faced growing competition from a variety of non-traditional companies. IPC believed these would start to drag down prices in the category. So in addition to strengthening IPC's brand so that it could command a premium position, it needed to reduce production costs.

Customer Vector: Traders are highly competitive and status-conscious, and the team found that the latest-and-greatest equipment would be prized — but only if it worked immediately. Traders have no patience for training of any sort — time is money.

Technology Vector: The long, narrow LCD screens on the old turret were expensive because they were custom-made, and they also looked old-fashioned because they were single color. For the IQ/MAX, they were replaced with off-the-shelf screens usually found in car dashboards, which were full-color, high-resolution, and provided a much better customer experience.

Challenge: Create a better usage experience for traders

Comparatives Vector: If you use a typical office phone at work, then you are aware that compared to even an inexpensive mobile phone most of them do less and are harder to use. Equipment on the trading floor is no different. As noted earlier, IPC realized that everyday consumer electronics were shifting customers' perceptions about the experiences they should demand in the workplace and from IPC's products.

Customer Vector: On the noisy floor, traders often missed pieces of calls. So the ability to replay the last twenty seconds of a conversation was built into the turret. Traders often helped each other out by covering one another's desks while one stepped away. To help the assisting trader understand which were the high-priority calls, the frog team had the turret display more information (caller name, which bank they belong to, and the like).

In the concept testing the team learned a lot about how traders parse their attention to different calls and other pieces of information they need to stay aware of, how they decide which handset to pick up, and how they prioritize waiting calls. This led to designing the turret with separate zones for different functions. To avoid distractions, the housing was kept monochromatic; all the color resides on the screens and matching-color LEDs on the adjacent button clusters. Attention to these ergonomic details helps traders quickly build habitual gestures.

Ease of use was paramount, as traders often receive only cursory training on the turrets, and may be unaware of even simple things like how to adjust the angle of the unit for better comfort.

Once design concepts were under way, two rounds of testing were conducted with traders in a realistic environment (not a bland focus group room) to get them to react to design variations and give feedback. These sessions were done with "appearance models" — physical models that looked highly realistic — and interactive demos running on actual touchscreens. The team also had them try out numerous button prototypes to find just the right combination of pressure and tactile feedback so that the traders could operate them with confidence.

Technology Vector: Traders work standing up and sitting down, so the new screens were selected for their legibility from many angles.

Sales Vector: The turret is obviously not a product found in retail stores; it is largely sold direct. IPC had traditionally sold to IT departments, whose priorities may be on price or the customer service agreement, for example, while the traders themselves may put a premium on how well the product helps them get their jobs done. By being able to demonstrate the drastically superior usage experience of the new turret, IPC opened the possibility to include head traders in the purchase process and make their needs part of the decision making.

Challenge: Understand how the turret fits into the suite of trader tools

Customer Vector: The turret is just one of several computers, monitors, keyboards, mice, and specialized terminals that crowd a trader's desk. The team designed the new turret to be a good "desk citizen" by making it smaller and allowing it to fit smoothly between existing keyboards and monitors. It also funnels all the other devices' cables behind it, keeping them out of the way. This decluttered the traders' desks and made them more manageable.

Talking with IT staff at trading firms, the frog team saw many broken phone handsets. Why? Because traders are rough with their equipment, often slamming handsets down or throwing them. Traders like to use the phone handset to hit the button on the turret that ends a call. So the button was made extra-sturdy to take the abuse, and its position adjusted on the turret to invite the habitual behavior.

Complementers Vector: Traders are surrounded by masses of screens displaying data, many of which have become standards in the industry, such as the data terminals provided by Bloomberg. These have established a visual language and patterns of behavior that could be leveraged for the IPC turret, reducing the learning curve for traders.

Challenge: Make the turret adaptable to an emergent future

Technology Vector: IPC's turrets have a seven-year life span, an eternity in high-tech terms, so the new product had to be flexible to meet unknown needs in the future. This led to the creation of a "backpack" module of electronics that could easily be swapped out for upgrades. For the new color screens the team had to find a vendor that could guarantee seven years' worth of supply to match the turret's projected life span.

Trends Vector: Communication demands on traders have increased dramatically in the last ten years as trading became more global and complex. The IPC turrets store hundreds of contact numbers, in addition to direct private lines to key contacts. All indicators were that demands for storage and complexity would continue to rise, making the backpack module additionally valuable since it allowed a longer turret usage life.

The collective impact of all these findings and design decisions was that the new turret exceeded all sales expectations. IPC achieved a 70 percent adoption rate in new pitches in the first year, a large improvement over the standard of 10 percent adoption for new IT products in the financial services sector.

Understanding Customer Needs

The vector that tends to absorb the most hours during synthesis is the one focused on understanding what customers want from the products they buy, use, and live with. How will the products fit into their lives, help them get activities done, and enable new activities and ways of living? What will the products contribute to their self-image and social and familial relationships? Combining these findings with ones from other vectors (as just described) is particularly important for developing core insights and focusing innovation efforts most effectively.

The most powerful customer insights are, like core insights, logical yet unexpected. If you are just coming up with bland statements like "make it easier to use," then you have not looked hard enough.

Unfortunately the vocabulary for describing what customers want is crude. The commonly used word *need* is not really satisfactory. It is too rational and sidelines the emotional aspects of choosing and using products. Distinguishing between a *need* and a *want* can be difficult. And needs are slippery and multi-layered; some are superficial symptoms and some are true underlying problems. To provide more finesse to thought on needs, it's useful to break them into two broad categories:

- *Functional needs* are needs around the customer's goals and the related capabilities required from the product. What utilitarian goal is the customer seeking to accomplish (for example, drill a hole, mount a shelf)? What performance issues must be addressed (does the hole get drilled the right size in the right place, does the shelf sit level, does the product last long enough to be considered a worthwhile investment)?

- *Experience needs* are needs around ease-of-use and quality of use. How easy is it to understand and use the product and extract the desired level of performance from it? How does the product make the customer feel? What status image does the product communicate to others, both during and outside of usage?

In creating a product we can satisfy functional needs but miss the experience needs, or vice versa. Satisfying one type of need does not automatically satisfy the others. IPC was already satisfying many of the functional needs of traders with its older turret, but by addressing experiential needs that made the utility more pleasant to work with in a stressful environment, IPC opened up new sales opportunities.

Within each functional and experience need are other aspects to consider: whether the needs are being met or not by current products, and whether the customers explicitly stated the need or whether it was hinted at or triangulated from multiple data points. These aspects break out into the two-by-two matrix shown in Figure 3.3.

Unmet needs tend to be of higher value to customers, and unstated needs are more delightfully unexpected when addressed. When you are able to determine an unmet need that customers are exhibiting but not able to articulate consciously (as frog saw with the stock traders who had developed workarounds to get equipment working the way they wanted, but did not explicitly state the root problems), then you have one of the most potent combinations of insights.

Not all needs are equally important; some go unmet and unstated because they are trivial. Not every unmet need is worth pursuing, or will attract customers or provide competitive advantage. Triangulating with all the tools in the immersion method will make it possible to find the most important needs, and also reduce the chances that competitors will be easily able to replicate the insights due to the complexity of analysis required.

FIGURE 3.3 User Needs Types.

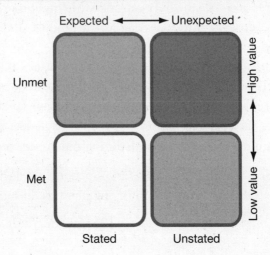

Stated and met needs must still be addressed (they probably reflect expected capabilities for the products), but by themselves offer less competitive advantage. That does not mean they should be ignored, however. They are useful for guiding specifics of product development, such as frog's finding that people disliked oven handles that poked kitchen guests in the back. This was not a big finding in itself, but it helped inform a larger design strategy.

Need-finding for product types that already exist and have precedent is fairly straightforward, as customers have a familiar frame of reference. What if you are aiming to make a product that does not yet exist, or you are not yet sure what the problem is you are trying to solve? In this case, it is wildly unreliable to ask customers directly what they want, and careful attention must be paid to unearthing unexpressed, unmet needs.

Recognizing Unmet Needs

One well-known company shook up the hidebound world of book publishing by seeing unmet customer needs and ignoring conventional boundaries of retail categories. Are you thinking Amazon? Guess again.

In 1935, Penguin Books came into existence because of a realization on a train platform. Penguin's founder, Allen Lane, was returning from a weekend with the famous mystery writer Agatha Christie, and looked in the train station's book stall for something to read on his journey back to London. Finding only popular magazines and poor-quality, luridly written novels, he wondered why there was not anything for the reader who wanted some good-quality fiction at a low price.[17]

Penguin Books began with a range of biography, crime-writing, and novels, all by contemporary authors and selling for a fifteenth of what hardback books usually sold for. Within a year, Penguin sold three million paperbacks by satisfying a need that traditional book publishers saw as off-limits. They were focused on a more upscale category, and assumed readers were warmly ensconced in a drawing room with plenty of time to spare.

After this initial disruption of combining high-quality content with low-cost production, Penguin continued to innovate. The German graphic designer Jan Tischold gave the books a consistent and striking design of two horizontal color bands sandwiching an off-white stripe. The color bands denoted the type of work—orange for fiction, for example—which helped customers quickly pick out what they wanted, and gave the books an unmatched brand presence in the stuffy, conservative world of English publishing. The basic design continues to this day. Penguin even experimented with a purpose-built dispensing machine for train stations, wonderfully named the Penguincubator (since penguins lay eggs), which, sadly, seems lost to the mists of time.

Innovate on Behalf of Customers

Some six decades later, Amazon did disrupt the world of book publishing and retailing. It has pioneered a number of capabilities on its site that customers never asked for, and in some cases disliked in testing, but that nonetheless went on to become major parts of the Amazon experience.

The automatic suggestion feature that prompts "People who bought this also bought that" was never requested directly by customers. But Amazon realized that people ask acquaintances for advice when making buying decisions offline, and modified the concept for online. Amazon's 1-Click feature, where purchases can be made with just a single click, met a lot of resistance when it was introduced in 1997, as online buying was still new for a lot of people at the time. But CEO Jeff Bezos insisted they give it a try, and it became very popular. Customers recognized and appreciated the convenience, which ultimately outweighed their concerns.

Maryam Mohit, VP of site development at Amazon, describes the process this way, "For us, it's a combination of listening really hard to customers, and innovating on their behalf."[18]

Interpreting and incorporating customer needs cannot be a mechanical process that is driven entirely by how customers feel today. Often radical innovation needs a push—get the concept out there and see how it works in the wild. (Later I discuss ways to do this in an iterative, risk-reduced manner.)

In *What Customers Want*, Anthony Ulwick argues, "Listening to the 'voice of the customer' has been the marketing mantra for more than twenty years, but it is time for that voice to be silenced. The literal voice of the customer sidetracks the innovation process because customers are not qualified to know what solutions are best—that is the job of the organization."[19] In other words, customers should be the inspiration for innovation, not the specifier.

Convergence

Convergence has emerged as one of the most important strategies for creating new growth opportunities, sustained competitive advantage, and the higher quality and more comprehensive experiences that customers are seeking. It can take several forms, as illustrated by these examples:

Amazon Kindle: As discussed in Chapter Three, Amazon constantly experiments with new kinds of offerings, stretching itself into sometimes unexpected areas. But while the Kindle electronic reader is Amazon's first physical product, it builds on the company's legacies in books, online retailing, and high-tech. Like Apple's digital media ecosystem, Amazon's offering is fronted by a device (the Kindle itself) supported by a background ecosystem. This systems approach puts it ahead of earlier e-readers from companies like Sony.

E-readers have been around for several years but have failed to take off into the mainstream. The Kindle has not yet hit mass appeal either, but it has addressed two factors that Amazon recognized as holding back previous efforts—buying books and then getting them onto the e-reader. The Kindle is fully integrated with Amazon's online store, making it possible to buy a huge number of books in its special file format, and do so with the same simple purchase experience that people are used to on the normal Amazon Web site. Second, Amazon arranged a deal with Sprint, the wireless carrier, so that the Kindle could communicate wirelessly with the online store. Using this feature, called Whispernet, Kindle owners can buy books on a whim—say, sitting in an airport lounge before getting on a flight—without having to go through a PC and then transfer the book over to the Kindle. The Kindle is essentially a disguised mobile phone, but the genius move was that Amazon did not force a monthly subscription on customers as a phone normally would—the cost is bundled into the purchase price of the e-books.

Levenger: This online and catalog retailer of premium stationery products lies at the opposite end of the spectrum from OfficeMax or Staples. Billing itself as "Tools for serious readers," Levenger offers a wide range of paper goods, pens, furniture, journals, and accessories for people who want something a little different for their correspondence or reading pleasure. In contrast to the Kindle, Levenger stands resolutely on the side of paper. (The CEO once wrote a blog post describing in intricate detail the sustainably maintained forest and paper mill in New York State that supplies some of the Levenger day-planner products.)

Levenger's prices are high compared to what you will find at the local office supply store, but its customer experience is a world apart too. The Web site is easy and crisp, and customers receive multiple e-mails giving status updates on their orders. When the products arrive they are often packaged in cloth envelopes, which in turn are inside custom-made, attractive boxes closed with a ribbon. Instead of a piece of paper just tossed into the box, your receipt is inside another envelope, along with a thank-you letter that recognizes if you are a return customer. It's all theater, but you feel like you got your money's worth. The products themselves back up the aura of quality by being attractive, well made, and built for years of use.

Consumer telecommunications: This industry used to be simple—in many countries just a single company offering only a single service, landline phone. What a contrast with today, where numerous companies compete with a wide array of services. Consider all the different products a telco (telephone company) offers now: landline, wireless voice, wireless data, text messaging, voice mail, ringtones, home broadband, television, and an ever-growing number more. These are delivered on a wide variety of devices for the home and on-the-go, very few of which are made by the telco itself. Then there is the back-end infrastructure:

the network, cell towers, billing systems, customer service, and retail stores. The traditional telco is also now competing against cable TV companies, start-ups offering Internet-based voice communications, and many niche wireless companies. Even Google is competing in the telecommunications area, with an operating system and various services.

Consumer telecommunications represents an extreme example of convergence. But many industries are shifting in a similar direction: automobiles, airlines, computing, insurance, media, and retail of all kinds, to name some. More and more, value is being created by integrated systems, not stand-alone products.

If done well, convergence helps you deal with two aspects of X-problems: It allows better and richer responses to customers' rising expectations (as Levenger does), and it allows you to pull together the necessary networks of individual components from across multiple domains, just as Amazon and the telcos have.

Defining Convergence

The term *convergence* has been used in various ways in recent years, such as convergent media, in which content is repurposed for use on TV, the Web, and mobile phones; or convergent advertising, in which two-way dialogue happens with customers alongside traditional one-way message pushes (such as people contributing self-made videos that become part of a larger advertising campaign).

Convergence as I am using it here means the integration of multiple products (hardware, software, and services) and customer touchpoints to provide functionality, benefits, and a customer experience that would be impossible in a stand-alone product.

As in the case of the Kindle and the telecom industry, convergence can combine products from multiple companies and can spread across industries that may at first seem separate. Some of the converged elements might be visible and used by customers, whereas others will be hidden but will play vital supporting roles.

Convergence can be very difficult to pull off well due to the level of complexity involved, the tight coordination across multiple organizations that is required, and the difficulty of creating a shared understanding of what you are trying to accomplish with the converged system, today and in the future. If done well, however, convergence provides a bulwark against competitors, simply because the difficulty of doing it successfully deters others. Complexity in this case is your friend, an enabler of competitive advantage rather than a foe to be minimized. A convergent approach has other benefits. It allows you to engage with customers in a richer and broader way, facilitating strong relationships and leading to measurably greater loyalty in terms of repurchasing, retention, and positive word-of-mouth.[1] If the right feedback mechanisms are in place, it allows a more thorough understanding of how customers want to use your products, leading to better products. And it provides the systemic underpinning that facilitates expansion of your business domain into new areas.

Touchpoints and Ecosystems

Companies often struggle to understand how to approach convergence in ways that will create value for them as well as their customers. A first step to successful convergence is understanding and controlling two related things:

- *The ecosystem:* The collection of products, technologies, and other components that together create the *functionality* of the offering. The Kindle's ecosystem consists of the e-reader device, the Whispernet communication network, and the online store. By any measure, the telecommunications industry is one of the most complicated ecosystems in existence today, requiring many different products from multiple companies to come together to deliver even the most basic capabilities for customers.

- *The touchpoints:* All the points where customer and company intersect over time, from a customer's becoming aware of the company's products to buying and using them. Collectively the touchpoints define the *quality of the experience* of the offering. Levenger creates and coordinates its touchpoints masterfully, giving it a premium position that is niche-oriented but highly differentiated from mass-market office supply retailers.

The goal with convergence is to make all the elements of an ecosystem and related touchpoints work smoothly together in order to provide a compelling experience that meets customers' needs, and creates a distinctive and defensible offering in the market.

Convergence Case Study: Maxtor and Touchpoints

Many companies see advertising as the most important means of communicating brand identity, but touchpoints play a role that is important and often more immediate and intimate. The product itself is, of course, a central part of the brand. Bruce Temkin of Forrester observes that great marketers focus on getting the product right. "This is because they know that great products and services, more than anything else, are the foundation of great brands."[2]

Focusing on touchpoints can bring benefits, even in a mature category that is highly technically oriented, as is the case with hard drives. Maxtor offers external hard drives used for giving extra storage space for a PC, or for backing up the PC's main drive (Figure 4.1).

FIGURE 4.1 Maxtor Hard Drive.

An external hard drive may seem like a straightforward product, albeit a technologically advanced one. In fact it is part of a system, and the manufacturers have not traditionally treated that system convergently.

Around 2004, frog design received a slew of similar proposal requests from all the major hard drive manufacturers: their external drive sales had flat-lined and they needed to figure out how to revitalize their markets.

All the manufacturers had hit the same wall: their products were better than what most people needed, at least based on technical criteria. They stored more than most people required, for one thing. When we interviewed customers we found that they averaged 140 gigabytes of storage — for an entire household — which is a problem if you are a manufacturer trying to persuade an individual to buy a 500-gigabyte drive. The drives were plenty fast and reliable. From a technical point of view, there was not much that could be improved. A race to the bottom on price seemed inevitable.

In working with one major manufacturer, Maxtor, research done by the frog team revealed that there were still considerable experiential problems with the drives, arising from a lack of a systemic approach to helping people choose, set up, and use hard drives. Focusing on these could differentiate Maxtor and stave off price commoditization. The goal became to create stories that customers understood, while taking the emphasis off of technology.

Maxtor had several key touchpoints which it could affect (shown in Figure 4.2).

The Hard Drive

The most prominent touchpoint was the external hard drive itself. Maxtor's previous drives were enclosed in cases of extruded aluminum that were functional but utilitarian. The frog team found that people wanted hard drives that were a better stylistic match with their desk-scape of flat panel monitors and consumer electronics. People also complained the drives were too noisy. To address these needs the team created an updated look that was distinctive and contemporary, and the new drives' rubber sides dampened sound and vibration as well as making stacking drives easier. The design was flexible and could be used on drives of various sizes with minimal cost penalties.

FIGURE 4.2 Maxtor Touchpoints.

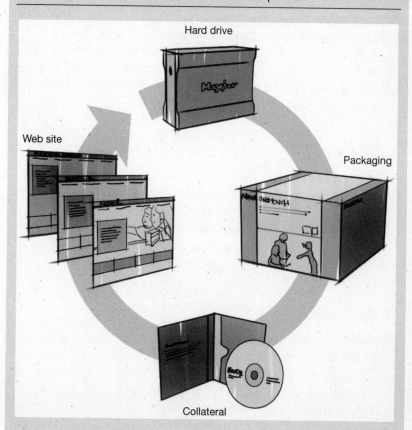

Hard drive

Web site

Packaging

Collateral

Backup Software

While the drives were the most prominent touchpoints, they were touched in a literal fashion infrequently after installation. In everyday use the software for backing up data took over as the primary touchpoint and face of the brand. Yet most drive manufacturers treated the software as an afterthought. Typically a third-party backup application was bundled with the drive, perhaps not even branded to match the drive itself, and was often confusing to use (which meant it wasn't used, and data went unprotected).

Maxtor also used a third-party application but had rebranded it, and had gone so far as to integrate it with the drive hardware, so that pressing a prominent button on the drive would initiate backup. Maxtor called this combination One-Touch, and it gained some advantage in the market by making the backup process easier. We further improved the usability of the software and redesigned the look of it to match the aesthetics of the drive cases, packaging, and Web site.

The Retail Store

Big box electronics retailers were a key channel for Maxtor's external drives. Drives were typically shelved in a corner of the store along with cables and other low-cost accessories — not exactly helpful for a brand trying to maintain a premium position. We knew that customers shopping for drives were largely on their own when it came to deciphering which of the options to choose, so a lot of attention was paid to the packaging and Web site.

The Packaging

With their historic focus on technical performance, hard drive companies were used to describing their products with exotic terms like "spindle speed" and "aereal density," which meant nothing to most consumers. Even gigabyte numbers were only vaguely helpful. So the retail box had to do a much better job of communicating the drive's value for the befuddled customer, especially given the uninformative retail environment. frog changed the language to more tangible units of measurement such as the number of photos or songs that could be stored. We added pictures of people (not the product) to engage customers emotionally. A strong color-coding system made the different types of drives easier to tell apart at a glance. We made the drive as easy to set up as possible, and continued the premium feel through to the internal packaging and manual.

The Web Site

Like most of its competitors' Web sites, Maxtor's was confusing because it tried to cater to both corporate buyers and consumers. The front page had a drop-down menu for finding a particular drive, but it was literally hundreds of items long, each described with a cryptic code. We created a micro-site dedicated to the new range of drives that was consumer- rather than corporate-focused. It had the same premium look and contained the same language and imagery used on the packaging, and provided better tools for customers to understand the differences among the various models.

Maxtor had not previously consolidated thinking on all these components and so had missed opportunities to solve customers' problems. By looking in an integrated way with a clear sense of how different drives should serve customers' unmet needs, Maxtor could connect with customers more powerfully. This is an example of how convergence can reap rewards when innovations on technical performance have lost their differentiating impact.

Maxtor is an illustration of how adjusting a variety of tangible elements made significant improvements to customers' perceptions of the company, its products, and the usage experience.

A common misperception is that customer experiences are ethereal and mysterious and therefore hard to control and consistently improve. Companies like Apple, Southwest Airlines, MINI, and Google, which turn out good customer experiences year after year, appear to have some sort of black magic. Nothing could be further from the truth. Customer experiences spring from concrete, controllable elements—the touchpoints. Good experiences result from a lot of hard work spent examining all the elements of the system and how they converge, and preemptively considering ways that the system can break or be used in unexpected ways. Companies that consistently create good customer experiences all recognize that they must pay attention to each of these concrete touchpoints and control them consciously and explicitly.

The fact is, your company creates a customer experience whether you intend to or not: those touchpoints will exist at the various stages regardless of whether you consciously control and integrate them. Chances are, the experience resulting from an uncontrolled agglomeration will be poor, or at least not as good and competitively differentiated as it could be. A clear understanding of the touchpoints gives insight into how a company is engaging with and supporting customers at all stages of their relationship, and provides focus for innovation where the relationship needs improving and customer needs are not being met.

There are two stages to this analysis. First, you create a *customer journey map* to understand the stages of relationship. Building on that, you create a *matrix* of the touchpoints themselves.

Customer Journey Maps

At the simplest level, a customer journey map is a linear, time-based representation of the stages that a customer goes through in interacting with a company. As with chicken soup, everyone has their own recipe, but a generally applicable framework is easy to state (shown in Figure 4.3).

(The figure will look familiar if you have used marketing funnels before. This is a modified version of that common approach to attracting and retaining customers by using marketing tools, but the focus here is on what customers are doing at each stage, not on how the marketer is pushing messages out to them.)

Engage: Engagement begins when customers first become aware of a particular need and start seeking a solution, or become aware of your or a similar product and have their interest piqued (after encountering

FIGURE 4.3 Customer Journey Map.

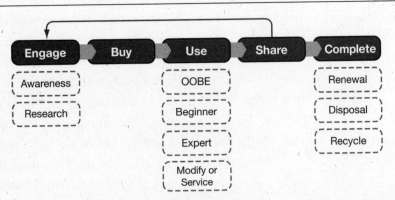

advertising, seeing the product, or hearing others talk about it). They begin researching the options on the market, assessing their needs and which options are the best fit. Research may be short (done in a single store visit) or protracted (I recall talking with one gentleman in Dallas who spent six months researching big-screen TVs, visiting stores dozens of times; he didn't want to get it wrong). Current customers will often be a source of input to prospective customers (hence the arrow running backward from Share). If necessary, break awareness and research into distinct stages and insert them into the top-level flow of the map.

Buy: The buy step is the purchase process itself, whether in a store or online. Often this step is outside the direct control of the company whose product is being bought, but the purchase process can be a good or bad first step in the relationship. When I bought my first cell phone, the registration process at the office supply store was so atrocious that it left a sour taste in my mouth that extended to the wireless carrier itself. For software or online service companies, the buy step is often under their control, and they have no excuse for not getting it right.

Use: After purchase, use begins. Many activities can fall into this stage and it may be necessary to break them out or do mini customer journeys for each. For example:

- Out-of-box experience: The initial unpacking and setup is now recognized as an important first connection point with a customer, and increasingly getting treated as a small piece of theater. Orchestrating it properly is itself an exercise in convergence.
- Beginner versus expert usage: Products are used very differently by beginners, as compared to experienced users who may want more functionality or shortcuts.
- Modification and customization: Some customers are willing and able to alter the product to suit their particular needs, or to upgrade or service it.
- Routine-based usage: Alternating routines of usage may occur that must be tracked separately.

Share: Once a user, each customer becomes an evangelist, a complainer, or an indifferent middle-of-the-roader. Those who are vocal become an influential input to the engage stage for prospective customers. Evangelists will likely renew; complainers will not.

Complete: This stage can have several paths that can be broken out separately: Becoming a repeat customer (or renewing a subscription), and disposing of or recycling the product. This final stage is becoming important in other ways as companies must increasingly be involved in taking back their own products and disposing of them or recycling them. Making this process smooth and efficient will bring cost and goodwill benefits.

These stages may apply to your situation, or you may need to modify them somewhat. As examples, here are some other variations that we have used at frog:

For health care services:

Motivation > Exposure > Commitment > First Use > Regular Use > Renewal

For an e-commerce site:

Site Landing > Product Discovery > Product Presentation > Shopping Cart > Check-Out

With the stages laid out, you can look at what is actually going on in each one and begin adding depth to it. Here is a useful set of topics to look at for each stage:

- *Motivations:* What are the customer's goals for the stage? For the engage stage, for example, Maxtor's potential customers are looking to either expand their PC's storage or to back up data from their main drive. If the drive will be used on a shared computer, the various end users may have different motivations that can affect the purchase selection.

- *Activities:* What activities are being done by the customer during this stage? During the research part of engage, hard drive shoppers may investigate the different drive options and manufacturers, read reviews, and try to learn the jargon and what the important differentiators are. Once they are using the drive, several patterns of activities may emerge, and different people in the household may all need to use the drive differently.

- *Questions:* What questions or concerns do customers have? Hard drive customers are often puzzled over jargon and specifications. They will also want to know issues such as manufacturers' reputations, products' reliability, and the best places to buy. Once they have bought the drive they may need advice on how to set it up.
- *Barriers:* What prevents customers from moving to the next stage? If they are overwhelmed by all they need to know, they may hold off making a purchase decision. Once they buy something and get it home, they may have problems setting it up properly, or getting the automatic backup working.

For each stage, list the motivations, activities, questions, and barriers on a chart like the one shown in Figure 4.4.

The journey map should be informed by insights into functional and experiential needs coming out of immersion so that it reflects actual customer behaviors rather than idealized or imagined ones. (Don't fall into the common trap of just treating needs as things that happen during usage—as with Maxtor, needs exist throughout the journey.)

Iterating the journey map *during* immersion activities as new data come in can also be useful, as it can prompt new avenues of investigation and allow real-time modification of hypotheses and concepts. A journey

FIGURE 4.4 Customer Journey Details.

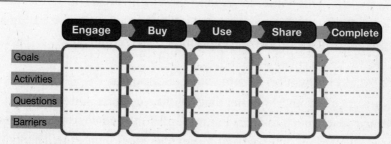

map can also be created on a new product concept so as to contrast the concept with the status quo and highlight where it is addressing unmet needs and tighten integration between stages.

Touchpoints Matrix

With the customer journey mapped out, you can move on to the next stage, creating a touchpoints matrix.

The journey map looks at things from the customer's perspective. With the touchpoints matrix you look from the company's point of view to see how you are supporting the needs of customers at each stage.

The matrix builds on the customer journey by listing relevant touchpoints at each stage as shown in Figure 4.5. Here are some generally applicable types, but again you may need to modify them for your situation:

- *Products:* The hardware, software, and services themselves. In Maxtor's case, this was the hard drives and the back-up software.
- *Interactions:* Two-way interactions that can be in person (such as in a store), on the phone, or virtual (Web sites, blogs, social network and user forum presences, and so on). Maxtor had relatively few direct interactions, and was reliant on others, such as store staff or current customers, to represent its products well.
- *Messages:* One-way communications that include brand, collateral, manuals, advertising, packaging, and the like. Maxtor's packaging and Web site were key messaging touchpoints that needed alignment in look and language.
- *Settings:* Anywhere that the product is seen or used: a retail store, a friend's house, TV product placement, events or shows. Maxtor's main setting was retail stores, but a prospective customer might see the drive at someone's home or office.

Focusing Innovation Efforts with Touchpoints

You can use your understanding of the customer journey and the related touchpoints to focus innovation efforts and conceptualize new product offerings. The goal is to create coherence for the experience both

FIGURE 4.5 Touchpoints Matrix.

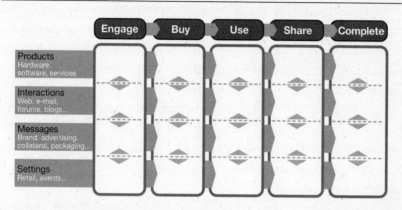

longitudinally throughout time for a given touchpoint, and also *vertically* for all touchpoints within a given stage. This creates a consistent story and personality for the entire ecosystem. It also minimizes the seams that inevitably exist between different elements, and that are the sources of so much customer frustration.

Looking at each element, ask yourself:

- Are the touchpoints addressing customers' motivations, and answering their questions or allaying concerns? Are they working for your target customers, and for novices and experts alike?
- Are the touchpoints addressing your customers' unmet needs, both functional and experiential? Are there unstated needs that neither you nor competitors are solving?
- Are all the touchpoints speaking with the same tone, the same message, even the same words? Is your brand being communicated effectively and clearly?
- Are there hiccups in the flow from one stage to the next that may cause potential customers to drop off, or cause dissatisfaction for current customers (and perhaps costly product returns or help-line calls)?
- Are the touchpoints differentiating you from competitors and helping retain the customers?

Defining an Ecosystem

While touchpoints are about the *quality* of experience that customers have while engaging with your company, ecosystems are about how a combination of components—hardware, software, services, underlying technologies, even multiple companies—come together to deliver the *functionality* that a customer actually uses.

Every company has touchpoints, but not every company has an ecosystem, at least to start with. Maxtor has a small ecosystem, just the drive and the software, but has quite a lot of touchpoints. On the other hand, telecom companies have very complex ecosystems combined with numerous touchpoints.

Even resolutely physical products that have traditionally worked in isolation can be reconceived in terms of an ecosystem. Nike has created an ecosystem around its shoes with Nike+, which integrates with an iPod, iTunes, and an online database and community, allowing runners to track their progress and interact with each other in an online community. As people run, their shoes (equipped with electronics) communicate to the iPod they are wearing about distance, speed, and calories burned. Upon returning home and connecting the iPod to a computer, runners upload the data, allowing them to analyze their progress and compare it with that of other runners on the same or similar routes. This has created a foundation that has transformed the running category for Nike. Nike Brand CMO Joaquin Hidalgo remarks, "Our revenue climbed as running became our fastest-growing category. And, more importantly, it showed us all how we could combine consumers' physical and digital experiences to create powerful new connections with our consumer."[3]

There are two basic questions to answer about an ecosystem:

• *What is the extent of the ecosystem?* What are the boundaries for what the ecosystem will accomplish? Often this starts out with one definition and changes over the course of development as the X-problem becomes better understood, and can change over years as the needs of customers and the goals of the company change. But at any given time the boundaries should be as clear as you can make them, and areas where the boundaries should be extended or retracted well understood. Otherwise, innovation efforts may clash with the boundaries.

• *What are the components of the ecosystem?* These can be diverse in nature, and again it is important to understand where your company wants to develop proprietary solutions and where you will integrate from outside. (There is a subtle difference between an ecosystem and a supply chain, in that a supply chain is generally defined as a sequence of processes and parts that *lead up to* a purchasable product. The ecosystem is what exists in order to serve the customer *post-purchase* on an ongoing basis. Each piece of the ecosystem may have its own supply chain.)

Ideally, an ecosystem and its components will be perfectly aligned with what customers want to achieve and the company's domain can deliver. Then customers are satisfied, and no resources are being wasted. (Note that this is not static however, so constant effort is required to keep the two in alignment.)

Case Study: The Zipcar Ecosystem

Zipcar has done an outstanding job of creating a complex ecosystem and coordinating a wide range of touchpoints.

Ten years ago, a number of car-sharing services were starting up in the United States, based on successful models emerging in Europe. Zipcar has gone on to become the biggest since acquiring its largest competitor in 2008. Zipcar now operates in twelve cities in North America as well as in London, England, and has a presence on more than a hundred university campuses.

Car sharing is an innovative way of reducing car ownership and environmental impact from cars. In essence, one subscribes to time in a car, rather than owning the car itself. For city dwellers (especially younger ones) for whom car payments, insurance, parking, and parking tickets can be prohibitively expensive, car sharing offers an attractive supplement to existing mass transit or bicycle. The cars may be rented for very short periods, just an hour or two.

Zipcar has converged an impressive ecosystem that is seamless for the customer. The ecosystem contains numerous components, which I describe in some detail to clarify the principles of ecosystem construction:

Cars: Zipcar stocks cars such as VW Beetles, Toyota Priuses, Honda Elements, and MINIs, as well as a few more upscale vehicles and task-specific ones like pick-up trucks. These cars all have a common trait: personality. And when you make a reservation, you reserve a *specific* car, not a class of car like "mid-size." Both differentiate Zipcar from a traditional rental agency, the land of anonymous vehicles. (Traditional agencies are starting to experiment with car sharing now that the model has proven itself, so it will be interesting to see whether Zipcar can continue to disrupt their business.)

Web site: This serves two purposes: first, to attract new customers, and second, to act as a reservation system for existing customers. The site allows people to identify car locations and availability (using integrated Google Maps), and make or change reservations.

Mobile integration: Cars can be located and reserved with mobile phones.

Back-end system: The Web front end is tied into a back-end system that handles billing and communications with the cars.

RFID card and reader: Upon sign-up, customers receive an RFID (Radio Frequency Identification) card that allows them to unlock and lock their allotted car. They wave it over a reader attached to a window. It will only unlock a specific car at a specific time, for a specific person. The reader is also tied into the car's central locking system and ignition system, so leaving the key in the car is not a problem.

Wireless network: Every car is wirelessly connected to the back-end system to allow communication of RFID permissions, customer unlocking, locking, and return, Global Positioning Satellite (GPS) data about car locations, mileage, and other information.

Parking spaces: To be useful, car-sharing services must have cars well distributed throughout their service areas. Zipcar negotiates sufficient spaces in convenient locations throughout a city, typically leasing them from an existing parking lot. Signs are erected to advertise the presence of the cars and prevent the spaces being taken by noncustomers.

Fleet management: Car selection and locations are load-balanced to meet local demand; utilization rates must be optimized for revenue and availability. (Zipcar has found that 40 – 50 percent utilization strikes the right balance — unlike an airline, the unpredictability of usage requires a lower utilization rate.) All the cars are serviced at regular intervals.

Car insurance: Provided by a third party, and included in the fees.

Policies: A communal service, in which many people share a common resource, is all about creating incentives for mutually beneficial behaviors without appearing so draconian that people are turned off before they even join. For example, there is a hefty fee if a car is returned even a few minutes late, since that can inconvenience the next customer.[4]

You will notice that many of these elements are quite mundane and in many cases hidden from customers' view entirely. But without them, the most obvious part of the system — the cars — would be worthless. The entire system has to work together for it to work well and deliver on its promise. Figure 4.6 outlines the whole system.

FIGURE 4.6 Zipcar Ecosystem.

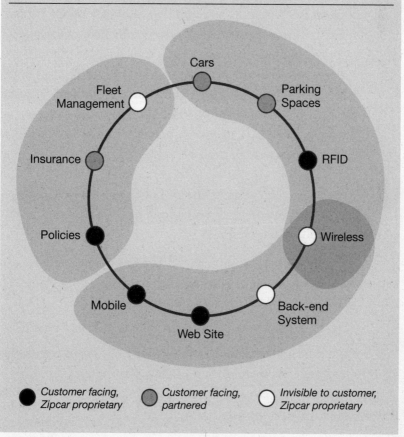

Zipcar has integrated three broad types of ecosystem components: physical, software, and service. These elements fall into four categories that apply across many other ecosystems:

- *Customer-facing elements:* These affect the customer experience directly and are visible to the customer, such as the Web site and the RFID reader.
- *Non-customer-facing elements:* These may or may not affect the customer experience but in either case are invisible to the customer. For example, Zipcar's parking space agreements are invisible and in themselves have no impact on the experience (though the parking spaces themselves do).
- *Proprietary elements:* The ecosystem creator develops components of the ecosystem that give competitive advantage or improve the product beyond what is available externally, or both. Zipcar's wireless communication with its cars is an example (though it is built on an existing cellular platform). Zipcar's founder, Robin Chase, presciently realized when starting up the service in 2000 that wireless technology would be key to success and invested a large portion of the starting capital in developing that infrastructure.[5]
- *External partner elements:* The creator develops formal arrangements with others to provide pieces of the ecosystem. Zipcar leases its cars, for example.

(Note that these are not mutually exclusive: external elements can be customer facing or not, as can proprietary elements, as Figure 4.6 illustrates.)

Focusing Innovation Efforts with Ecosystems

You can use your understanding of the ecosystem to focus your innovation efforts and conceptualize new product offerings.

In creating a new ecosystem from the ground up, you should be concerned with questions such as these:

What Are the Goals for the Ecosystem?

At a high level, what is the ecosystem going to do, and what components will be needed to deliver it? Do you need to own all aspects of the ecosystem, or can you carve off a specific footprint and allow others to fill out the remaining parts? Can the ecosystem be built in stages, or is it so interdependent that it must all be made at once?

Since you are dealing with an X-problem you will rarely find a single answer for the goal at the outset of establishing the ecosystem. It will take several iterations to arrive at an answer that balances the numerous interrelated issues: customer experience and needs, competitive differentiation, cost and risk of development, capabilities in your company toolbox and what you will need to source from outside, speed of development, ability of your organization to manage the complexity, and so on.

How Will the Ecosystem Affect Touchpoints?

How will the functional capabilities of ecosystem elements affect the experiential qualities of specific touchpoints? In the case of Zipcar, Robin Chase and her team would certainly have put much thought into the step of a customer arriving at the parking lot, identifying the specific assigned car, and unlocking it. There are multiple ways this could have been handled from a functional and technology perspective, each with pros and cons over the chosen method of signage and RFID. You want to have a thorough understanding of all the options and be able to make an informed decision about how they affect development cost and risk, the usage experience, competitiveness, and so on.

What Can We Learn from Others?

How have competitors set up their ecosystems? What have companies in other industries done that we could learn from? Using some of your immersion tools, you should gain a competitive baseline and see what lessons you can draw from comparatives. In particular, pay attention to how companies have chosen to specialize in a category of components (physical, software, services), and which components they have made proprietary or have partnered on. Are there ways that you can take a different tack that will allow you to better address customers' unmet needs, or provide cost or future development benefits? Could you take advantage of untapped technologies or partners that have been ignored by customers?

Maxtor recognized that improving the software component would bring customer and competitive benefits, and made the effort to develop outside its core hard-drive arena. Zipcar retained control of most customer-facing components, while partnering on many non-customer-facing ones. However, it saw wireless communications as a key enabler and chose to develop that feature independently. Even though it was not a customer-facing piece of the ecosystem, it offered cost and fleet management benefits that competitors would find hard to replicate.[6]

Improving an Existing Ecosystem

When you have an existing ecosystem and you are seeking to converge it more effectively, there are additional issues to consider:

- Which components are responsible for which touchpoints, and how are they contributing to problems and opportunities identified in the touchpoint matrix analysis?
- Based on customer needs, competitive analysis, and strategic factors, what functionality do you need partners to be enabling in their components?
- Should your partners be visible to your customers in the end product? Sometimes third-party ecosystem elements cause confusion, as was the case with hard drive backup software (which is why Maxtor submerged it under its own brand and experience). In other cases it can be beneficial, as is the case with Apple having prominence in the Nike+ ecosystem.
- Will you gain more from addressing customer-facing or non-customer-facing components? While not as glamorous, improving back-end components can have big payoffs in the quality of experience and operational efficiencies.

- Are there opportunities for expanding your capabilities from one category (say, hardware) into another (say, software or services)?
- Are there opportunities for expanding your reach so that you take over ownership of a component that is currently provided by a partner? This may allow greater integration or superior functionality.

When looking at convergence of an existing ecosystem, the conversation can quickly slip into divergence: Which areas would be best to expand into? How can the ecosystem grow to provide more capability? I return to these issues in more detail in Chapter Five.

Ecosystems Are Hard to Converge

An acquaintance of mine who is a big steam train buff once took a vacation to the small town of Wolsztyn, Poland, to visit the last remaining section of steam railroad still running in Europe. Poland modernized to diesel and electric trains some years ago, but an English train enthusiast by the name of Howard Jones persuaded the Polish government to set aside this section of track to preserve the wonders of steam. Enthusiasts can go there and actually drive the trains for a few days as part of a program called the Wolsztyn Experience.

People get very passionate about steam trains (especially my fellow Englishmen, who comprise 90 percent of the visitors to Wolsztyn). There is something highly visceral about steam power: the sound, the smell, the moving parts that propel the enormous engines. Today we are used to technology working invisibly or microscopically, so it is startling and refreshing to encounter a machine that seems so alive. Steam locomotives are enthralling to everyone.

You don't find so much interest in railroad track, switching stations, or running schedules, however. The trains (especially the locomotives, even the diesel ones) get all the attention, but they are useless without the ecosystem that makes them worthwhile for paying customers. Trains as a product are interesting—but worthless. But trains as part of an ecosystem are tremendously valuable.

Ecosystems have tremendous benefits, but converging them successfully is often very difficult to do. The reasons for this come down to
some qualities that are inherent to many complex systems.

Ecosystems Can Be Hard to See

Products tend to be tangible (whether physical or digital, you can "get
your arms around them" conceptually or literally). But ecosystems can
involve a lot of invisible and less glamorous components that make
them hard to understand, and therefore difficult to work on. Often
these are connective elements, like train schedules or switching stations,
that make the more prominent products work together. Customers tend
to experience the system through the figurehead elements and take the
less visible connective tissues for granted.

But you cannot afford that luxury in the design process; often it is
the invisible, boring things that make or break a product.

Years ago at frog we had a client who, like Zipcar, was starting a
car-sharing service. Its focus was Atlanta, whose notoriously bad traffic
made the plan to rent cars for short periods to complement existing
mass transit seem like a good idea.

The client's choice of car did not look like such a good idea,
however. It wanted to use a Smart Car, which is now available through
mainstream Mercedes Benz dealers, but back in 2001 was only available
in Europe. This meant it had to go through U.S. crash certification, an
expensive and lengthy process likely to require significant reengineering
of the car.

Furthermore, it wanted to use an electric version of the Smart
Car—which didn't exist anywhere on earth. It would have to be
developed from scratch. Obviously this presented certain difficulties,
not least of which was a collection of electric charging stations that
would have to be sprinkled at strategic points throughout Atlanta.
Beyond that, the ecosystem would need to be built out to include many
of the same elements as Zipcar's does today.

The company staff had focused almost all their attention on the
engineering for crash testing and electric conversion, but had largely

ignored other important factors, including how customers might use the service, how things might go wrong when renting an unfamiliar electric car, how the end-to-end service experience would work (signing up, making reservations, returning the car), how to load-balance the fleet across the city, how to manage maintenance, and so on.

Hogging the spotlight like a steam train, the product was getting all the attention while critical ecosystem enablers were left unattended.

Ecosystems Are Fragile

Ecosystems contain many elements that must work together. The ecosystem is only as strong as its weakest link. Seemingly small faults can ripple through to have large unintended consequences, just as annoying mismatches in train schedules disrupt the larger usage experience. One of the most complex and confusing ecosystems that regular people may come into contact with is home theater. Anyone trying to assemble a moderately sophisticated home theater (such as a television, receiver, surround sound speakers, cable or satellite box, DVD player, and cabling) is going to be immediately assaulted with massive numbers of acronyms, technical jargon, unfamiliar specifications, and competing standards for such things as surround sound and picture quality. The standards are so plentiful and so often incompatible that sorting through them to put together a system that *just works* is an almost masochistic exercise.

It is a bad sign when you find multiple online forums dedicated to unraveling the intricacies of your ecosystem. Here is an excerpt from one forum post (don't worry if it looks incomprehensible—it does for 99 percent of people):

> For HD and Blue Ray DVD HDMI audio I do not understand if any post processing is done on the 5.1 Lossless PCM channels from these players. Will DD PLIIx or THX 7.1 apply to these? What are the limitations?
> If I have a 1080P video stream going through the unit with HDMI to my display device, how does the OSD and Set up menu display?

This is not an unusual post. Forums are filled with highly technical questions such as this as prospective customers try to come to grips with all the mismatches of components in the home theater ecosystem that stand in the way of the whole working together. There is no excuse for subjecting ordinary people to this level of complexity when they just want to purchase and enjoy the equipment.

Ecosystems Cross Organizational Boundaries

Ecosystems often necessitate collaboration of disparate organizational groups (even multiple organizations) because each contributes to the customer experience. This makes them an administrative nightmare and exacerbates all the tensions, insecurities, and divergent directions within an organization. Getting ecosystems to work well and come alive from a customer experience perspective often takes a certain spirit of benevolent dictatorship. Steve Jobs's enforcement of a unified vision has contributed to Apple's success at establishing coherent ecosystems to deal with thorny X-problems.

Convergence and Sustainability

The imperative to create products that are more environmentally sustainable presents some interesting convergence challenges that will become ever more pressing in the coming years. Sustainability is increasingly a competitive differentiator, as well as becoming necessary for regulatory compliance. Knowledge of how to achieve sustainability in a given industry will be a prized capability.

Today sustainable products often cost more and work less well than disposable alternatives; they may require different behaviors from customers, and even the most sustainable products are still a long way from truly having zero environmental impact. As with any other area of product performance, this is a ripe area for innovation. Achieving this means multiple capabilities and company divisions (and external partners) will need to converge in order to bring the systemic approach that sustainability requires.

For example, HP was able to dramatically reduce the quantity of packaging it used for bulk-shipping millions of desktop printers each month from assembly plants to distribution centers, at the same time dropping attendant costs and transport-related damages. Kevin Howard, the HP engineer who pursued this approach, says, "We found that when items are boxed, people have the tendency to throw them around or run into them with forklifts. Boxes actually invite damage. So we eventually decided instead to ship products without one." The printer engineers worked with Howard early in the design phase, and found that adding a few ribs to the interior of the printer housing allowed the surrounding cardboard box to be removed. The refrigerator-sized bundle of printers could be held in place only by trays that sat between the layers of printers, a solution that would have been impossible without collaboration across groups.

An additional surprise was that the packaging innovation had benefits beyond resource reduction. Howard observes, "Our damage rates decreased, our loadability increased about 2.5 times, and we began to save significantly on transport costs."[7]

Thinking sustainably also expands the notion of the customer life cycle, and puts more emphasis on the "complete" stage than is typical. Companies are being required to take responsibility for taking back and reusing, refurbishing, recycling, or disposing of products, or finding ways to extend the life of products through maintenance and upgrades. Treating this systemically and convergently rather than haphazardly will lower costs and improve customer satisfaction. Dell and HP, for example, have both taken significant steps to help customers return old laptops and (in the case of HP) inkjet cartridges with a closed-loop system that is easy to use.

At the product end of the spectrum, the complexity of the manufacturing ecosystem will increase as new technologies (along with new vendors) are brought online to lower environmental impact. More attention will need to be paid to such things as usage and waste of energy and materials, and toxicity reduction and containment. Companies will have to think carefully about which of these can be outsourced and which should be developed internally for competitive advantage.

Finally, sustainability can point in new business model directions, such as converting products to services, or switching from selling to leasing products. As with Zipcar, these have to be treated very differently from traditional one-person-one-product ownership models, and success depends on taking a convergent approach to the whole experience and back-end system.

o   o   o

Convergence helps deal with several aspects of X-problems: having to deliver integrated systems rather than stand-alone products; increasingly demanding customers who want higher-quality, more seamless experiences; creating differentiation in competitive markets; and making innovation efforts more effective by setting boundaries and defining focus areas.

The point of convergence is making existing ecosystems and touchpoints work better. What if you find gaps in them, or want to expand into new areas? That is where our next topic, divergence, comes in.

You may have noticed that in many of the examples convergence was happening in parallel with divergence. That is why convergence and divergence lie opposite one another in the Innovation X diagram—they are complementary but opposing forces.

Divergence

I n the 1990s, Brita, well known for its water filtration pitchers, was facing a decline in customer demand. The problem was not competition from other pitchers; Brita dominated the category. Rather, Brita's pitchers were in competition with two completely different products: bottled water, and refrigerators with water filters and dispensers built in.[1]

Bottled water from companies such as Calistoga, Arrowhead, and Aquafina became very popular at this time. Packages of plastic bottles by the dozen started showing up in big box retail stores like Costco and Walmart. Parents loved them because they were convenient to carry around and keep in the car.

Simultaneously, large refrigerators with built-in water filters and dispensers in the door had become the must-have kitchen appliance in suburban housing developments. To make matters worse, two of Brita's key traditional pitcher competitors—PUR and Culligan—had locked up co-branding deals that gave them the majority of the U.S. refrigerator market.

Brita had an X-problem: the pitcher category would not go away immediately, but unless the company could find a way to establish new value with customers it faced a margin-squeezed death march as the market dwindled.

X-problems occur most frequently at times of volatility and transition such as Brita experienced. It is at such times that the divergence method of the Innovation X framework becomes important. Several paths may present themselves, but each has upsides and risks that are hard to quantify ahead of time. Divergence is about seeking out new customers within your existing market and appealing to them in new ways, finding new markets to expand into, or expanding your footprint in the ecosystem to deliver products in new ways.

During these periods, it becomes harder to say what the domain of your business is. Long-held truths about who your customers are and what their needs are get called into doubt. Understanding adjacent domains is also harder because, although they may be tempting areas for expansion, their very adjacency means they are often suffering the same shock waves of volatility.

If you picture the common industry S-curve diagram, shown in Figure 5.1, X-problems happen primarily at the two ends, where there is the most volatility and where questions of divergence are most pressing.

At the bottom of the curve, a new product category is still in chaotic and fragmentary formation. The X-ness of this period means the category's defining factors are still unknown: who the customers are, what exactly the products should do, how people will use them, and who the competitors will be. Start-ups are often specifically geared for this stage of a category, and take bet-the-farm hunches on the answers to the X-problem. But for an established company in another area, the question is whether to diverge into this potentially lucrative new category.

FIGURE 5.1 Industry S-Curve.

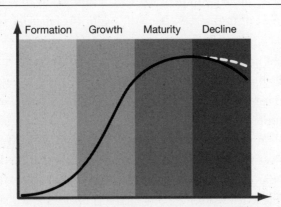

As the dimensions and vital characteristics of the category become clearer, and the value proposition engages with more customers, the category ideally takes off into its growth period. At this point, many companies enter the fray, and often there are acquisitions of category pioneers by larger firms looking to get a piece of the action.

The middle of the curve is more stable. At this stage the category has matured, the players are largely set, new entrants are few and far between or are small and exploiting niches, the customers are known, and innovation is largely incremental. X-problems are less common or are smaller in scale, while complex problems (where the problem is known but the solution is not) dominate. The emphasis is on creating cost efficiencies and customer loyalty. Growth continues but over time shifts to taking customers from competitors, rather than from net gains of market size. This stage can last a very long time—the car industry was in the stable middle of the curve for eighty years and only since the 1990s has it crested the top, at least in developed countries where the market is saturated. But these days the happy middle tends to be shorter rather than longer.

At the top of the curve, X-problems occur when a stable company gets disrupted by new competitors diverging in from unexpected directions. Often a new category, chaotic and unfocused, challenges the primacy of an existing, highly focused one. For a time, these live side by side until they shift to coexist, or one displaces the other. There are several choices at this stage: ride it out and stave off the end as long as possible (surf the dotted line cresting off the top of the curve); join the disruption in some fashion; seek out other areas entirely (perhaps by jumping onto the bottom of another emerging category S-curve); or pursue some combination of these. Facing these choices, Brita opted to pursue the "ride it out" strategy without dramatic changes to its products. It was fortunate that an environmentally fueled backlash against bottled water emerged, prompting customers to once again look at Brita's pitchers, but if that had not occurred then more radical steps might have been necessary.

Mapping the Domain

A first step in divergence is to understand what you are diverging *from*. For that you need to have a clear understanding of your business domain.

As stated at the beginning of the book, thinking about your business in terms of industries and categories can limit possibilities and cause a blinkered view of competitors, leaving you open to unexpected new entrants and disruptions. A more flexible mind-set is that of *domains*, a term advocated by Gary Hamel in *Leading the Revolution*. A domain can be thought of as the playing field available to you. Too often companies see it in an overly restrictive and constrained way, focused on a product-, category-, or market-centric view. Your customers do not see the world through the lens of your product lines; they see it through the lens of their needs.

By defining the domain more concretely, you can see the true dimensions of the playing field and new areas to expand into.

Hamel only gives a brief description of the concept, so here I'm going to formulate it somewhat differently and build on it, tying it into the analytical tools discussed so far.[2]

A company's domain consists of three things, shown in Figure 5.2.

FIGURE 5.2 Domain Elements.

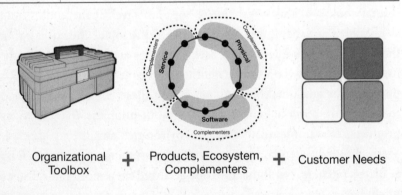

Organizational Toolbox + Products, Ecosystem, Complementers + Customer Needs

Organizational Toolbox

This term describes the collection of capabilities and knowledge at your disposal in multiple ways. This includes your core competencies and capabilities, core insights, IP and proprietary technologies, driving values, brand equity, past experiences, and past products or product concepts.

This can be your starting point for thinking about a divergence, or it can be a check against the other divergence approaches to see what you can pull off. But toolboxes are not static: you can generate or seek out new tools to open up fresh options.

Products, Ecosystem, and Complementers

Collectively this area covers the products and product lines you make, how they are integrated with other products (yours or others'), and complementary products (shown in the diagram extending outward from the three ecosystem categories of physical, service, and software products). If you are a maker of products that are not, and will never be, part of an ecosystem, then you will have a series of disconnected points, but each will still have a related cloud of complementary products.

Whereas products that lie within your ecosystem are part of the integral functioning of your offering, complementers are products that are bought or used alongside your products but do not contribute so closely to their functioning. For example, someone may buy a printer to print out photos from a digital camera, but the printer is not critical to the camera itself, as photos can be acquired multiple ways. Likewise, online photo sharing sites and drug store printing services would be complementary to the camera, while custom software to extract photos from the camera would be part of the ecosystem. To take HP as an example once more, it extended its ecosystem into the complementary areas of online photos and drug store printing in an effort to integrate those more tightly into its ever-widening digital photography ecosystem. It added to its toolbox in the process.

(As discussed earlier, a company can expand its reach over touch-points also, outside of ecosystem changes, but this does not typically have a significant effect on the scope of the business domain. An exception is when companies extend their footprint into direct retail, as Apple, Dell, and Sony have all done, for example. When touchpoint changes coincide with business domain changes, they are usually driven by shifts in a company's place in the ecosystem.)

Customer Needs

Enabled by your toolbox capabilities, your products and ecosystem address the various kinds of customer needs (functional and experience, met and unmet, stated and unstated). For divergence it is vital to take a needs-based view of your customers rather than a more traditional demographic segmentation approach. If your products meet needs for some current customers, it may be fairly straightforward to satisfy that same need for some very different customers. By the same token, if there are unmet needs for current customers, focusing innovation efforts there could lead to an expansion of your domain.

Think of toolbox and customer needs in the familiar technology-push/market-pull framework. With your toolbox capabilities you can find ways to push into new areas, and unmet needs create a vacuum that pulls in new solutions. Necessity is the mother of invention, as the old saying goes, and unmet needs are an opportunity to create a new product or improve an existing one. But understanding customer needs should underlie any divergence effort, regardless of whether it originates with a rethinking of your toolbox, products, ecosystem, or complementary products.

You will have been building up the necessary knowledge with immersion and convergence to define your domain comprehensively. Virtually all the immersion research vectors will be applicable, along with the ecosystem-mapping and needs-analysis from convergence to complete the picture.

You can use the knowledge you have to identify promising areas for innovation.

Toolbox-Driven Divergence

The collection of knowledge, capabilities, and past experiences that companies acquire over time can be used to extend their domains in sometimes surprising ways.

The online shoe retailer Zappos is known for its outstanding customer service, efficient order fulfillment, and playful in-house work culture. It is experimenting with extending these toolbox capabilities into some unexpected areas. With "Powered by Zappos" it is syndicating its end-to-end experience system, including product browsing, buying, and post-purchase support, for other online retailers to use. And with "Zappos Insights," it is disrupting expensive management consulting firms by offering perspective and advice about how to create a customer-service-focused company. For a minimal fee, small business owners can visit the separate Zappos Insights site, pose questions directly to Zappos staff, and read articles about how Zappos approaches many aspects of its business.

Zappos is leveraging its toolbox in admittedly unconventional and radical ways, but you should constantly be thinking about how to extend your IP, brand, insights, and capabilities in new directions. You may not act on them right away, or at all, but continual practice will keep your organization sharper when it does come time to make a move.

Here are some questions to consider when thinking about a toolbox-driven divergence:

- Is your current toolbox limiting the needs you can satisfy for your customers? Conversely, is there IP in your toolbox that could satisfy needs that are going unmet now?
- Do your core insights point to unstated and unmet needs that you could be addressing, or to new product, market, or experience opportunities?
- Does your brand have the necessary stretch and permission to expand in the desired direction (will customers see the move as credible)?

- Are there other product categories to which your capabilities, brand, technology, or IP could be applied?
- Are there past "failed" products, concepts, technologies, or experiments that can be brought back to life in a new context?

Complementary Products Divergence

Here you want to take a broader view of the activities that customers pursue around your products, and see what other products (hardware, software, or services) they use alongside yours. You may uncover opportunities for products that address customer needs that you are only partially addressing currently. Furthermore, complementary products may offer ways to attract previously unreachable customers. Keeping an eye on complementers may also highlight companies you need to keep an eye on, either for acquisition or because they may be candidates for divergence into your domain, turning them into direct competitors.

Some questions to consider when looking at complementary divergence:

- Are there other products customers are using alongside yours that you could also produce, or combine their functionality into your products?
- Are there markets adjacent to yours that companies see as distinct but customers treat as one? Or are there products in adjacent markets that would benefit from integration across market lines to make the products work better?
- Does your brand have the necessary stretch and permission to expand in the desired direction (that is, will customers see you as credible in the new market)?
- Do your core insights provide guidance on market opportunities that a more superficial understanding of customer needs or market boundaries may disguise?

- Are there other markets in which your toolbox of capabilities, technology, or IP could be applied?
- Are there emerging cultural, social, usage, buying, or economic trends that are creating opportunities for expansion?

Logitech and Continual Complementary Divergence

Logitech, a maker of computer peripherals, has repeatedly diverged into complementary product areas. Its core products are mice and keyboards, of which it is one of the two dominant manufacturers along with Microsoft. But it has diverged into a variety of other related categories, in large part out of necessity as almost every category it enters gets quickly commoditized. Keyboards, mice, webcams, computer speakers, video-game controllers . . . all started out as fairly expensive devices with decent margins. Each slipped into price wars as the markets got saturated with competitors vying for shelf space and customer attention.

Within its wide portfolio, Logitech must therefore juggle both higher-margin products at the early stages of category maturity and others in very mature categories with extremely slim margins. Not an easy trick to pull off.

Even in the highly commoditized mouse and keyboard categories, Logitech has not been afraid to explore new upper reaches of price. It has introduced premium keyboards and mice with beautiful craftsmanship and materials and innovative interaction capabilities. This creates a halo effect to its lower-end products, as well as giving more price headroom to the category.

Logitech pursues complementary divergence by addressing evolving customer needs within a category, and also by creating new product categories for brand new types of needs and customers.

Expand Product Capabilities

Logitech was one of the first companies to make computer mice, and over time it has created a broad range of them with increasingly sophisticated features that align with customers' changing usage.

The first mice were very simple, just a couple of buttons on a mouse attached by a cord that used a rubber ball for motion sensing. Over time, mice have grown in technical performance through a number of innovations such as using lasers to detect motion, scroll-wheels, buttons for controlling the computer's speaker volume, dedicated buttons for Internet search, and lots of customization options.

Logitech saw opportunities to move beyond mice designed for general audiences. It created mice specifically for video gamers, who have more demanding needs (and more price flexibility) than average customers. The gaming mice incorporate higher-precision motion sensing, weights to adjust how the mouse feels in the hand, and buttons specific to gaming. Logitech now also makes mice specifically for laptop customers, with features like wireless sensors miniaturized so they are not so bulky protruding from the computer, and lower profiles so the mice more easily fit into laptop bags.

New Product Lines

Logitech is no longer just a PC accessories company. It has a variety of products that go head-to-head with offerings from traditional consumer electronics manufacturers. Beyond mice and keyboards its product lines now include webcams, remote controls for home theater systems, joysticks and other gaming controllers, home security systems, and audio-related products for iPods and PCs. Most of these are stand-alone products that do not require sophisticated integration into complex ecosystems, and Logitech does little to try to force customers to buy other Logitech products through proprietary interfaces.

With two recent acquisitions, however, Logitech has branched into more ecosystem-heavy products. Logitech acquired a company that makes sophisticated universal remote controls for home theaters, called Harmony, and a company that makes a device known as Squeezebox for wirelessly connecting a PC with a music library to a stereo system. In Harmony's case, the ecosystem is wholly owned by Logitech: a PC application interface connected over the Web to an online database of home theater components, to which the remote is connected via the PC and programmed. With Squeezebox, Logitech is piggybacking on an ecosystem anchored by Apple's iTunes and iPod.

It's necessary to understand your strengths when diverging.

Having as diverse a portfolio as Logitech can lead to loss of focus for a company. As John Hagel and John Seely Brown argue, "Without some sense of long-term position, movement rapidly degenerates into random motion.... Companies lacking a sense of direction usually fall into reactive approaches, pursuing too many options at the same time. The result is that resources are spread too thinly and performance impact diminishes because all the initiatives are under-resourced. In times of increasing uncertainty and rapid change, reactive approaches can become significant traps."[3]

Diverging into complementary products requires an understanding of how you are going to address needs in a new way so that you can differentiate yourself from incumbents. But Logitech's success shows that it is also important to have a clear understanding of your values, your priorities, and what you bring to the table. Logitech's product line is varied, but a closer look reveals some clear criteria that have guided its divergence:

- *Focus on products that involve human interaction.* Hands-off products like wireless routers, for example, would not be a fit for Logitech.
- *Look for categories that are just emerging from the bottom of the S-curve and are poised for mainstream growth and maturity.* Logitech is not a pioneer of categories, but it is very good at sensing possibilities and getting in early. It can also use its design, manufacturing, distribution, and marketing prowess to thrive in the mature middle.
- *Find opportunities for innovation,* particularly in the areas of customer experience, design, ergonomics, and technologies that Logitech is familiar with (optical, ASICs, sensors, micro-controllers) or unfamiliar ones that do not require large R&D investment (such as software design).[4]

Not every category has to be a mass category. Logitech has some fairly exotic products, like specialized devices for controlling 3-D computing environments. But Logitech can make products work if they fit specific criteria: demanding users who will pay a price premium, product life cycles that are not annual or fad-driven, and enough of a market to support them without requiring large marketing effort.

Did Logitech start out years ago with these principles? Unlikely. It takes time to discover a company's strengths and weaknesses, always through a process of trial and error (adaption). Just as customers have a hard time articulating their unmet needs, companies have a hard time distilling what they do well. It is often not until a divergence works or, perhaps more important, fails that a company discovers where its true competencies lie. Like a rock climber, you have to fall off before you realize your limits.[5]

Some of Logitech's divergence guidelines could be considered core competencies, such as knowing how to spot a promising new product category and jump in at just the right time. This doesn't involve *technological* competency, but it is a valuable capability nevertheless, and Logitech's consistent success at it cannot be just chance. It is an example of what I call *pattern experience,* a topic I cover in more detail in Chapter Eight. Through skill or happenstance, certain people in the organization acquired expertise at the pattern of finding emerging categories, were able to apply it repeatedly, and passed it on to others informally or through codification.

Ecosystem Divergence

Whereas divergence from the organizational toolbox seeks out new markets for current capabilities, ecosystem divergence looks for ways to encompass a larger footprint within an existing ecosystem. This often entails encroaching into the domain of another company and causing your ecosystems to overlap in ways that put you in new head-to-head competition. For example, Oracle has traditionally been purely a software company focused on corporate databases, but its acquisition of Sun Microsystems has given it capabilities in enterprise servers, data storage, and operating systems. This ecosystem expansion has put it into direct competition with companies like HP and IBM who were formerly just partners in delivering other elements of the overall networking ecosystem.[6]

Often the easiest way for a company to expand its reach within the ecosystem is to take on development of components that lie within the same scope as its existing offerings. A company that makes hardware will generally have an easier time making new hardware products elsewhere in the ecosystem, and a service company will be better set up to deploy more services than to launch a hardware product. These routes of least resistance are often the best first place to look for ecosystem expansion possibilities, but they are also easiest to replicate by direct competitors. Shifting sideways into another realm of the ecosystem and taking on very different capabilities to create new kinds of offerings is harder, but provides a stronger bulwark against competitors trying the same thing.

When considering an ecosystem-based divergence, ask yourself questions such as these:

- Are there unmet needs that your customers have that are being caused by gaps in the ecosystem, or that could be satisfied by expanding the ecosystem's capabilities?
- Are there holes in the touchpoints matrix, or problems in the matrix, that stem from components of the ecosystem? Are there areas where you should take more ownership?
- Do your core insights tell you more about what an ideal ecosystem should look like than is revealed by a cursory understanding of customer needs?
- Are there products being used alongside yours that you could also produce, or functionality you could absorb into your products?
- Are there other products that are unrelated to yours but used in the same context?
- Should the new capabilities be organically developed internally, or should you acquire them from the outside?

The issues around ecosystems are complex. Three case studies of companies in different industries will show how ecosystems can be approached in different ways and present new opportunities and challenges: Alltel in wireless communications, Pure Digital in consumer electronics, and Progressive Insurance in automotive insurance.

Alltel — Divergence from Services to Software

In the complex world of mobile telecommunications this kind of sideways shift is becoming common. One example is Alltel, a midsize carrier that sat between the large national carriers and the smaller regional, niche, and prepaid service providers. Alltel did not have the R&D or acquisition clout of the big players, and it could not be quite as nimble or low-cost as the smaller ones. It needed to find a way to differentiate itself while playing to its strengths.

frog had done several projects with Alltel, and in this case it turned to us with the open-ended challenge to help them find a sustainable competitive advantage, and to increase data usage. The result was a product called Celltop, which was a new approach to bringing a widget-type interface to the phone (now more familiarly seen on smartphones like the iPhone). Instead of the usual menus with multiple levels and choices, Celltop presented the phone's owner with a display visually split in two, with each half displaying a different nugget of information, such as the local weather forecast, or a list of recent text messages. These could be scrolled through so that a variety of different widgets appeared. Clicking on one of the widgets caused it to expand and reveal more detail.

Celltop was an instant hit with customers, and as a result they started using data services much more. By making relevant nuggets of data more immediately available and easier to work with, Alltell increased data usage on its network significantly. Furthermore, Alltel expanded its system view to encompass the Web: customers could download new widgets on a PC browser and make other customizations, and these would be synchronized over the air with their phones.

Developing Celltop required a significant divergence for Alltel. Software development was not in its organizational toolbox, and it took some time for its people to learn how to integrate it into existing processes. They had never done Web integration with their phones to this extent either. But by expanding their reach into these challenging areas, they achieved several things:

- Defensible differentiation from the smaller wireless players (who were highly commoditized and cost-focused)

- The ability to develop the interface in response to emergent customer behaviors at a nimble pace that larger carriers with longer development cycles could not replicate
- An answer for customers' frustration with different interfaces across multiple handset manufacturers' phones, which were often complicated to use for simple data-related tasks

Pure Digital — Changing Ecosystems Based on User Needs

A company that has both created a new ecosystem (as Zipcar did) and subsequently needed to change it dramatically is Pure Digital. Pure started out making inexpensive digital cameras with one ecosystem, and then had to significantly adapt its approach when it began producing camcorders.[7]

When was the last time you pulled out your camcorder? I'll wager it has been ages. And how long since you sat down to watch footage you shot? Probably even longer. That would make you quite typical.

The camcorder is possibly the world's most popular gadget that gets very little actual use. Rather than step back, and wonder why, manufacturers like Sony, JVC, and Panasonic have happily continued along their conventional paths, larding on more and more features, bigger lenses, and more buttons than a jetliner cockpit. They are all stuck in the land of feature creep and have forgotten why people want to use camcorders in the first place: recording their memories, reliving them later, and sharing them with others.

During research efforts at frog, we talk with many people about their use of digital technology, and will often ask about camcorders. The reaction is sometimes one of surprise—"Oh! I forgot I had that!" and the interview subject will pull out the camcorder and dust it off like a vintage wine. But most people we talk to just don't bother with them anymore.

One woman in Minneapolis admitted that whenever she reached for her camcorder, the fuss of charging the battery, finding fresh tapes, and carrying the bulky bag were just too off-putting. She wanted shooting video to be quick, easy, and not distracting from the event itself. Instead, her camcorder was fighting spontaneity with every fiber of its being. So she left it at home and just used the video mode on her digital "still" camera. The quality wasn't as good, but it was fast to use, she already had it with her, and the file sizes were small enough that she could easily share them with friends and family without having to deal with complex editing and video compression software. She could transfer the video straight from the camera to an e-mail message or Web site.

Many people buy camcorders for one reason: the arrival of their first baby. They start shooting a lot of video, but then haven't got the time to do anything with it.

Camcorders appeal to people who want to capture memories, but clearly the assumptions driving camcorder development have been out of step with what most people *really* need.

Pure Digital has taken a very different tack that zeroes in on these unsatisfied needs: spontaneity, sharing, and ease of use. In contrast to the dogged complexity of the mainstream consumer electronics brands, Pure's rallying cry is "The simpler it is, the more fun it is." It has gone on to become the fastest-growing Silicon Valley company, with an astonishing growth rate of over 44,000 percent from 2003 to 2007 (that is not a typo).

Pure Digital started out making very low-cost digital cameras — digital equivalents of disposable film cameras — and from the start took an ecosystem approach to the problem that many people had of getting photos off their digital cameras and being able to share them easily with others. Pure partnered with a number of drug-store chains to create a closed-loop system that replicated Kodak's original "You push the button and we do the rest" philosophy for the digital age. Customers would take their cameras full of images into the drug store, which would "process" the images and give them back on a CD. The camera itself would return to Pure for refurbishing and reuse.

A few years later, Pure introduced a low-cost camcorder in a similar vein. Its video quality was relatively poor and it only held thirty minutes of video, but its price was only about $30. Pure positioned it not as a camcorder replacement but as a step up from the disposable camera market (which shipped 218 million units in 2004). It had many of the same attributes as disposable cameras — cheap (thanks to tumbling prices of solid-state RAM and other internal components), lightweight, simple, and ideal for use by kids or in adverse environments like a beach.[8]

That first Pure video camera was part of a similar retail-store-based ecosystem that extracted customers' video and put it on DVDs (the fee for which allowed the cheap up-front cost in a razor/blade model). But Pure discovered that this model did not work so well for video. Customers wanted to keep the camcorders as it took longer to shoot thirty minutes of video than it did to fill up the digital still camera. So the company shifted gears and relaunched the camcorder, now named the Flip, as a stand-alone device that could transfer video directly to a PC.[9]

The ecosystem then expanded in another direction: software. Pure realized that one of the biggest hurdles for people was doing light editing to their videos and then sharing the results with family and friends. It created a proprietary software application that resided on the camcorder itself, so that when customers plugged the device into a PC, they could launch the application (without the fuss of installing anything) and use it to edit, combine, and then share their videos by e-mail or by posting them on a Web site. (Pure has benefited from the parallel rise of sites like YouTube.)

Additionally, Pure launched a sophisticated Web site that allowed people to customize the appearance of their Flips before purchase, using thousands of available decorative patterns and images, as well as uploading their own photos to put on the outside of their new Flip.

The Flip and its follow-on models have propelled Pure into a 24 percent share in the overall camcorder market, second only to Sony, and it is the leader in solid-state camcorders. Today Pure sees itself as a software company that does elegant hardware, which makes it the opposite of a company like Sony.

Pure's founder Jonathan Kaplan observes, "Creating something simple and fun is very hard; it's not easy. Otherwise everyone would be doing it." He goes on, "Traditionally, consumer electronics companies were focused on creating the smallest, coolest and most technologically advanced products, but they came at it from the hardware side. We came at it from the ecosystem side, meaning that there's great software that resides in the device and on the computer and on the Internet. And the combination of those three things creates an ecosystem that has a lot of value. Our belief is that great software is going to create great consumer electronics."[10]

Pure's ecosystem approach and emphasis on software as a source of cutting-edge customer experiences were clearly a key reason for Cisco Systems to acquire Pure in 2009. Cisco has been expanding beyond its core area of enterprise networking and moving more solidly into the consumer realm, and Pure's capabilities will be a strong asset in Cisco's integrated future.

Progressive Insurance — Establishing New Ecosystem Components

Pure Digital shows the value of expanding an ecosystem's boundaries and components (not just one's reach within an established ecosystem, as Alltel did). Pure first created and then adjusted its ecosystems in response to unmet customer needs, allowing it to disrupt two fairly mature categories: digital cameras and camcorders.

Similarly, Progressive Insurance has gained ground against more established insurers by expanding the conventional ecosystem for car insurance in several ways that have obvious and also hidden benefits. First, Progressive uses its Web site as a means of attracting and serving customers. (The site famously quotes competitors' rates, for example, and is the main interaction point for customers, rather than agents in offices). Second, Progressive has a fleet of white vans that are dispatched to help customers at the scenes of accidents. Both of these new ecosystem components came about through rethinking how to address unmet customer needs. But they also provide Progressive with competitive advantages that may not be immediately apparent.

Car insurance is a cruel business, in which customers regularly shop around to find the best price. They rarely have to use their insurance, and mostly when they interact with an insurer it is because of something unpleasant, such as paying the monthly bill or dealing with an accident. Without a continuous stream of positive interactions, flight of customers to other insurers is an ever-present risk. So why would Progressive encourage potential customers to go to other carriers (the price comparisons), or add costs to its services (the vans)?

In addition to being a delight for customers who find themselves in a stressful car accident, the vans actually save Progressive money. Fraudulent claims are frequent with auto insurance, so by sending a representative immediately to the scene of the phoned-in incident, Progressive can verify that it has truly taken place. This curtails fraud at the source rather than dragging it out over weeks and incurring large legal costs. Each representative in a van is equipped with a laptop and a wireless connection back to the company's database, allowing more efficient gathering and input of data from the field. Progressive has invested heavily in wireless and IT and developed many custom systems; its IT staff has grown from a few hundred to several thousand in the last decade and is a core part of the company's toolbox in a way unlike that of any other insurer.[11]

Quoting competitors' rates is a more subtle ploy. Customers love the convenience of one-stop shopping for quotes, so Progressive is doing them a favor. But Progressive is not always the low-price leader — in fact half the time it isn't offering the lowest quote. So why let potential customers know? Because Progressive believes that it is more accurate than other insurers at gauging a specific individual's risk and setting premiums based on it. If the customer chooses Progressive, then Progressive has covered its costs. But if, as the competitive quote may encourage, the customer chooses a lower-priced carrier, Progressive has sent that costly and risky customer to a competitor. Very clever. The customer self-selects not to join Progressive, yet walks away with a positive feeling and will likely try Progressive again in the future.[12]

This case study of Progressive shows the advantages of a thorough analysis of one's domain that aligns toolbox capabilities with ecosystem scoping, building on both of those as necessary, and underpinning efforts with insights about unmet customer needs.

o   o   o

Divergence often goes hand-in-hand with convergence, as with Alltel and Maxtor: diverging into new areas of capabilities opened up new ways of competing and new markets, but also entailed greater integration of touchpoints or ecosystem elements.

The lines between toolbox-, ecosystem-, and complementary-driven divergences are often blurry, and even from the examples given it is clear that there are interrelated issues in each. The three are not mutually exclusive approaches; one can be pursuing a strategy that is a combination of two or three. But by separating them out I hope that you come away with a clearer understanding of the different divergence options, and what it takes to be successful in each as you solve your X-problem.

6

Adaption

It is not the strongest of the species that survives, nor the most intelligent, but the one most responsive to change.
—CHARLES DARWIN

The Toyota Prius has become *the* icon of the environmentally responsible lifestyle. But it has done so in spite of being worse than conventional cars—slower, uglier, more expensive. In fact, the premium price of the Prius over conventional economy cars—including ones made by Toyota itself—does not justify the improvement in fuel savings. Meanwhile, Honda's hybrid efforts have had much less market and brand impact. An adaptive approach to emerging opportunities, based on a close reading of the market, has made the difference for Toyota.

As we race to avert the potentially catastrophic effects of global warming, we are moving from a gasoline monoculture (to put it in agricultural terms) to a world with a diversity of coexisting alternative fuels. Electricity, hydrogen fuel cells, natural gas, diesel, and hybrid combinations of them will all have their place.

Toyota and Honda have both made impressive advances in hybrid gasoline/electric drivetrain technology, reminiscent of the lead Japanese automakers took in producing parsimonious fuel-sippers in the wake of the gas crisis in the early 1970s. This will benefit them in the years to come as environmental regulations intensify, customers demand better fuel efficiency and lower environmental impact, and the alternative fuels become widely available.

Both companies have introduced hybrid drivetrains in a variety of models. Toyota's core Prius model has far exceeded sales expectations. In 2006 Toyota sold almost as many Priuses in the United States as Volvo sold of its entire line.[1] In Berkeley, California, Priuses were at one point making up fully half of the Toyota dealer's sales.

Early on the customer acceptance challenges were considerable, as the first hybrid vehicles were underpowered and overpriced compared to their conventional competition. Deciding how they would position the new vehicles to attract customers must have been a vexing question for Toyota and Honda. Both introduced initial seed vehicles to test reactions (Figure 6.1). As results emerged about how the vehicles were liked and used, and what the market reception was, the two manufacturers pursued more full-throttle approaches, but did so in very different ways.

Honda created a quirky initial vehicle, the Insight, a small two-seater with space-age looks aimed at pioneering customers who would be drawn to (or put up with) its iconoclastic design. It actually came out in the United States before the Prius and achieved superior fuel economy. Nevertheless, it sold far less than Honda had hoped for, only 18,000 over its lifetime.[2] By contrast, Toyota sold over ten times that many Priuses in 2007 alone.

FIGURE 6.1 Honda Insight, Toyota Prius.

Toyota Prius First Generation

Honda Insight

Toyota Prius Second Generation

Honda soon switched to an approach of integrating the hybrid powertrains into conventional Civic bodies, which paradoxically meant its most advanced technology powered its budget line of cars. This led to two challenges in the market. First, budget-minded Civic buyers saw the hybrid model as too expensive (and for relatively little return on investment, since the gasoline-engine Civics already had very good gas mileage). Second, for those buyers more interested in the status symbol of cutting-edge hybrid technology, the impact was lost because the first hybrid Civics were virtually indistinguishable from their conventional brethren.[3]

The first-generation Prius, introduced in 2001, was the result of a massive engineering effort going back to the early 1990s. Due to the novelty of the design, all the critical engineering aspects—drivetrain, batteries, vehicle structure, manufacturing processes—were interdependent and had to be created in parallel.[4] This was unusual for Toyota, which normally operated in a more compartmentalized manner.

The company set a target of 100 percent fuel efficiency improvement over a similar non-hybrid Toyota, a jump large enough to support the price premium necessitated by the substantial development costs. Toyota also wanted to ensure that the Prius would not get quickly leapfrogged by competitors.

Project leader Takeshi Uchiyamada recalls, "I thought we had to choose the most efficient technology in order to become a leader in hybrid cars. As an engineer, I did not want to choose an easy technology that would allow us to introduce hybrid cars to the market first, but might be replaced by superior technology later. Besides, I thought the cost would come down as Toyota was very good at reducing cost." Uchiyamada wanted to invert the normal flow of carmakers responding to regulation by *anticipating* the future and developing products that would create new markets.[5]

That first Prius was more conventional than the Honda Insight in packaging (it carried four people with good luggage space), but its aesthetics were equally polarizing. In my opinion it was not at all attractive, but it was distinctive and practical, and that was enough for the pioneer buyers, who placed a premium on fuel efficiency and reduced pollution.

Toyota recognized that the second-generation car had to appeal to a wider audience than the pioneering eco-conscious buyers. The challenge was how to sell a car that by most conventional measures—speed, handling, interior space, aesthetics—was "worse" than a normal car, yet cost more.

Learning from its experience, Toyota did several things for the second generation:

• It positioned the car as a social statement, and smartly built on a groundswell of public enthusiasm. One survey revealed that more than 50 percent of Prius owners selected "It makes a statement" as the main reason they bought the car.[6] Toyota benefited from celebrities such as Leonardo DiCaprio showing up at red-carpet events in their Priuses rather than limos.

• It did not position the Prius as a budget product (as Honda did with its Civic hybrid), but rather as a higher-end car.

• In keeping with this positioning, Toyota added luxury features like high-intensity headlights, satellite navigation, integrated Bluetooth, and keyless entry and engine-start. The Prius dashboard looked like a videogame, with large color LCD screens that lovingly displayed the inner workings of the car's hybrid engine. The screens were used for another high-end feature, a camera to aid seeing backward when reversing the car. These helped justify the higher price and delighted customers who were either moving up from economy cars or moving down from premium cars, attracted by the Prius as a social statement.

The Prius as Hero

My colleague Phillip Vasquez has observed that Toyota created a "hero's journey" for the Prius: it became the plucky underdog that overcame its weaknesses to triumph in the face of adversity. Buyers were able to bask in these heroic qualities and feel like they were part of a larger movement. Toyota's advertising campaigns cleverly played up the "We're in this together" image.[7]

Prius owners became very attached to their cars and would go to extreme lengths to extend their capabilities to even more heroic levels. A trend of Prius-hacking emerged as people explored ways to improve mileage to over 100 mpg, and to get the complex computers and screens inside the car to do nonstandard things—be a display for a small Mac computer in the dashboard, for example. Some people sought even better mileage by converting their Priuses to be rechargeable from electricity at home rather than charging while driving, something Toyota itself has resisted.

Ultimately, Toyota did roll the hybrid powertrain into its more mainstream models, including luxury vehicles in its Lexus division. While Honda dropped the Insight nameplate, Toyota maintained the flagship Prius, which provided a focal point for the hybrid technology message. (Not coincidentally, Honda reintroduced the Insight name after a few years' absence, again with a very distinctive look that resembled . . . the Prius.)

Honda treated the Insight as a technology testbed and then rolled the technology into a wider array of existing models more quickly than Toyota. (Arguably, from an environmental point of view, the better approach.) Toyota saw the Prius not just as a technology trial balloon but practically as a sub-brand, and crafted a broader set of attributes around it that aligned with the company's emerging understanding of who wanted to buy the car and why.

By iterating multiple elements of the system (the car exterior and interior, the marketing, how it addressed user needs, the hybrid technology itself) based on the emerging social context and experiences with the first-generation model, Toyota was able to create a strong lead in a strategically important new category.

Adaption to Deal with Emergence

I have always liked the following quote from John Chris Jones, an early pioneer of formalizing product design processes, which acknowledges the inherent ambiguity and interrelatedness of problem and solution when tackling complex challenges:

> The fundamental problem is that designers are obliged to use current information to predict a future state that will not come about unless their predictions are correct. The final outcome of designing has to be assumed before the means of achieving it can be explored.... The instability of the problem is what makes designing so much more difficult and more fascinating than it may appear to someone who has not tried it.[8]

This encapsulates why the emergent nature of X-problems makes them so difficult. The problem you are trying to solve is not fully or even partially defined at the outset, and the very act of solving it uncovers new dimensions that were previously unknown. In some cases, the problem itself can change *because* of the solutions you have created.

Like evolution, adaption is about continually evolving to thrive in a dynamic environment.

This requires several capabilities:

- An ability to perceive the environment as it is today, predict how it is changing, and spot opportunities, threats, and areas where you are not ideally suited (missing on customer needs, wrong system model, gaps in domain capabilities, and the like)
- An ability to be flexible at responding to changes in the environment with new products, adjusting your mix of capabilities and partners as needed
- A feedback loop to see whether the changes have made you better or worse adapted than before

Earlier chapters have looked at how to be successful in the first area: building a thorough understanding of the emerging context, finding opportunities within it that can be used to focus innovation efforts, and spotting unexpected threats. All are critical capabilities for planning strategy and developing a product. But they are equally important once a product launches. Only then can you see how your experiment works in the real market and what new aspects of the X-problem are revealed.

If you fail to stay immersed after the launch, then you miss out on critical information that can guide future efforts.

In this chapter I take up the two other factors: flexibility during development, and establishing feedback loops between the changing environment and your development organization.

Flexibility

A manager I once worked with had a sign above his door: "Everything changes." In an X-problem world, the only constant is change.

When facing rapid and continuous change and high levels of ambiguity and risk, flexibility is a valuable characteristic. Flexibility lets you leave your options open and put off decisions until as much information as possible has been gathered to inform them. (This is not the same as procrastination, however, where decisions are postponed even when adequate information is at hand.) Early on, as you are coming to grips with the X-problem, you need flexibility to deal with the rapidly changing understanding of the problem, what the opportunities are, and hypotheses about how to proceed. Over time, as the X-problem becomes better understood and more manageable, you can become less flexible. And at some point flexibility must disappear so that you can ship a product. That does not mean that flexibility cannot live on in parallel, however, by getting shifted to next-generation or related efforts.

Flexibility during development is becoming a cornerstone of progressive companies, who are turning to a variety of approaches.

- *The use of simulations throughout the development process for physical products.* In the 1990s Boeing attracted much attention with its boast that it did not build a single physical prototype of its 777 plane, instead relying solely on 3D software right up until production. Whether or not that was literally true, today it is common practice to do a lot of computer simulations early and often in development.
- *The use of rapid prototyping in the development process for physical products.* Despite the success of simulations, physical

prototypes have a real role to play, and in recent years, various computer-driven prototyping methods such as 3D printing have become available at low cost, making highly accurate and functional prototypes more available than ever before early in the process.

- *On-demand manufacturing.* On-demand manufacturing has pushed flexibility into the supply chain, pioneered by Japanese automotive companies, and by Dell in computers. This practice diverts as much responsibility (and risk) as possible to contract manufacturers and other partners, freeing the developer to focus on a smaller set of issues.

- *Agile programming.* This method of software development canonizes flexibility into core principles: produce code that is highly modular and reusable; avoid lengthy specification or requirements documents; rapidly prototype code and use frequent customer feedback to make adjustments.

Open-source software and, as mentioned, Google's approach of keeping new services in beta mode for long periods (four years and counting for Gmail) are essentially never-ending prototyping efforts that take as a premise the need for flexibility and constant change. Being flexible assumes that you will get things wrong at first and acknowledges the emergent nature of the problem. Prototypes give you the necessary early feedback and warnings if things are astray, allowing early and frequent course-corrections.

Rapid Systeming

It is common practice to do rapid prototyping of individual hardware or software products, but in a convergent system context it's necessary to think in terms of iterating the whole system in a coordinated and integrated way so as to understand its behavior and the total experience it will deliver for customers. I call this approach *rapid systeming*.

The system you are seeking to rapidly iterate consists of your domain and the controllable touchpoints with your customers. That is to say, the content of the frameworks discussed in Chapters Four and Five.

Collectively these include:

- Hardware, software, and service products (as an ecosystem or as distinct entities)
- Customer-facing and non-customer-facing ecosystem components, and ecosystem components made by others
- Customer needs (obviously you do not control these, but you can experiment with addressing them in each prototype)
- Complementer products (depending on how tightly in step they need to be with generational changes to the core product)
- Touchpoints (some you will control directly, others you may want to influence, such as retailers)

All elements of the system should be treated in an iterative and flexible manner. All can be adjusted over time as the X-problem becomes better understood, with careful attention to cascade effects between them. Not all system elements need be changed for every iteration, but there must be enough coordination of related elements that they can deliver a coherent customer experience.

Managing rapid iteration development within a product itself is hard enough, but it becomes exponentially more difficult when extended out to the broader ecosystem and third-party vendors, and includes consideration of how these all intersect with emergent customer needs, core insights, and emerging opportunities. Multiple business units, divisions, and departments in your organization must be aligned on focus areas, goals, deliverables, processes, and time lines.

Rapid systeming should be practiced during development, but should also be continued after the launch. In an X-problem world, every new product launched is essentially asking customers, "How does this work for you?" Each product release (with its attendant system) should be seen as a hypothesis that can be shown partially or fully incorrect, in which case a course correction is required. The most reliable information about the X-problem comes back after the product reaches the market, and you should adjust your approach to future development accordingly.

FIGURE 6.2 One Innovation Effort Informing Another.

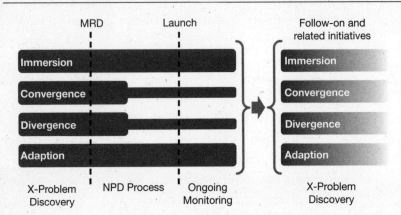

Figure 6.2 builds on the schematic time line diagram in Figure 2.2. Here a follow-on effort is shown to reflect the fact that one innovation or product initiative must be used to inform next-generation and related efforts.

There is extensive research and literature about approaches for flexible product development (but for isolated products), continuous improvement between generations of products, and continuous learning when doing iterative releases (agile programming, Kaizen for production processes). So far as I am aware, no one has yet given a term to an iterative approach to convergent systems. In my work at frog I see companies experimenting with ways to do it, recognizing the need, but they lack a name for it and well-defined approaches. We are still in early days of understanding how to accommodate the conflicting demands of large systemic complexity with rapid iterative change in the face of ambiguous goals.

Nevertheless, there are some lessons from existing approaches that we can apply. I will draw from the principles of agile programming, as well as the extensive writings of Preston Smith and Donald Reinertsen on this issue.[9]

System Architecture

Reinertsen calls architecture "the invisible design."[10] He is referring to how elements of a physical product are divided up and oriented to one another (for example, laptop and desktop computers are two architectures adapted for different purposes but with much the same functionality). In a convergent context, the architecture is how a company organizes the hardware, software, and services elements, along with collaborating partners and perhaps complementers. Zipcar created an architecture for its offering that is suited to the experience it wanted to provide, and that matched its internal capabilities and allowed it to safely draw from outside without harming its customer experience or competitive differentiation.

There are several major considerations about architecture choices:

Proprietary and integrated versus standard and modular: Consider which elements of the architecture should stay proprietary, and which ones can be outsourced, or taken from preexisting components. Is a highly integrated, custom-optimized architecture necessary to deliver the desired performance, or will it be possible to assemble from readily available modules? Toyota chose a highly integrated architecture for the Prius, with all elements developed concurrently to optimize the performance of the car.

I cover this topic in depth in Chapter Seven, but for now suffice to say that early in the life of an X-problem, a highly integrated approach is often required. As the problem stabilizes and the needs and constraints become clearer, you can shift to a more modular architecture based on standardized components.

Capability location: Just as in a physical product, where specific functions can be shifted around between architectural elements (for example, the power supply in a desktop computer is inside the main housing, but is part of the cord on a laptop), the dividing line between hardware, software, and services can move dramatically. In many high-tech products today functionality is increasingly getting shifted from physical controls (hardware) to on-screen controls (software). "Cloud" data services like Gmail and online photo storage have shifted customer data out from the traditional location on the PC, opening up new usage and revenue opportunities (e-mail access from anywhere, easy sharing of photos for print purchasing).

Match to customer needs: Consider what the customer will be seeking from the total system in order to decide the optimum location for specific functions, rather than simply assuming that a given function must live in a certain architectural element. For example, some mobile phones in Europe do not have built-in address books. How do you find your contacts to dial then? The phones pull the customer's MySpace or Facebook contacts off the Web in real time (an example of the cloud approach). This is convenient for customers, as they do not have to duplicate contact information across multiple devices, and the address book suddenly becomes very rich in its capabilities.

Front-load changes: Changing architectures late in a development cycle is often difficult (though they can evolve across generations). So complete all experimentation with system architecture configurations as early as possible, with as clear an understanding as you can achieve at the time about the ramifications of your choices. Explore ways to segment the architecture broadly (such as the three main chunks of hardware, software, and service) so that they can be iterated internally with minimal impact to the rest of the system.

System Decoupling

The notion of *decoupling* covers a variety of ways of reducing risk, fostering flexibility, and allowing concurrency of development. Decoupling elements of the system means that changes in one do not overflow into another, causing instability in the system as a whole.

Standardize Interfaces

One way to wall off unstable elements is to standardize an interface between the volatile element and other elements of the system. This means that changes in one do not affect the other, because the inputs and outputs between the elements are known and stable. For example, the hardware elements of the system may need to be locked down earlier than the software ones, due to longer production lead times. Establishing rules about how the software and hardware interface with one another will allow the software to continue to evolve while the hardware shifts into production preparations.

This is a well-understood principle in both physical product and software application development. For example, APIs (application programming interfaces) provide the standards for external developers to build on core applications to enhance their functionality. The ease of integration of Google Maps has turned it into a far more popular platform than online maps from Yahoo and Mapquest that preceded it.

The iPod dock connector is an example of a standardized hardware interface—it has stayed consistent almost since the very first iPod. This has allowed a vibrant universe of complementary products to spring up around it, with the only variation being adaptors to accommodate the various size iPods.

But Apple is not perfect: with its App Store, where iPhone users can buy third-party applications, Apple has exasperated developers with opaque and seemingly random rules about which applications are permitted in the store and which are not. The band Nine Inch Nails created an iPhone app that was rejected due to "objectionable content," even though music from the same band is downloadable on Apple's iTunes music store. Almost at the same time, an application that allows frustrated parents to blow off some steam, so to speak, by shaking an animated baby on the screen was accepted (though subsequently pulled after fully justifiable public outcry). Other developers feel like their applications are rejected because they tread too close to Apple's own software plans. Variable "standards" are a sure way to degrade momentum, and if developers don't know until they submit their applications for approval whether all their hard work will come to fruition, Apple risks alienating them and seeing its system stumble.[11]

For IPC's trader turret, it was unclear what the future would hold as far as communication technologies such as Voice over Internet Protocol (VoIP) that the turret would have to interface with, or how the high-resolution screens would be used as new services became available. So the hardware was designed with modularity in mind—with the aforementioned "backpack" of internal components that could be swapped out easily, and the unit itself designed in several function-specific modules so that changes in one would not affect the others.

Don't Overanticipate

With X-problems, it is not always easy to tell what to standardize early on, how stable those interfaces will be as the problem definition changes, or even what constitutes dividing lines between different elements of the system where interfaces can be created. At the very earliest stages of tackling an X-problem, overanticipating interfaces can actually be detrimental, either because they require up-front cost and coordination to develop that may be wasted, or because they may prematurely lock in architectural decisions that prove limiting in the future.

This brings me to a principle of agile programming—YAGNI: "You aren't going to need it." This means you only build into the code what is immediately necessary, and you avoid overcomplicating the software by trying to anticipate future customer needs that may never come to pass. In agile programming, this goes hand-in-hand with a continuous process of simplifying and modularizing code as much as possible, so that new and unanticipated capabilities can easily be added later.

Preston Smith notes, "When change is rampant, YAGNI embodies considerable wisdom; when relative stability prevails, ignoring the future is foolhardy, especially when high cost-of-change items, such as architectural choices, are at stake." He goes on to say, "The opposite of YAGNI might be IMNIL (I might need it later). This might be the wisest choice in certain cases.... However, you will only know by comparing the costs of change against the more subtle advantages of keeping the design simple for future changes."[12]

The Internet bubble flop WebVan, which pioneered Web-based ordering and home delivery of groceries, is a textbook example of overbuilding in anticipation of customer demand that never material-izes. It burned through so much cash building out proprietary, highly advanced automated order fulfillment systems that it could not survive the slower-than-expected adoption rate.

On the other hand, sometimes underanticipating can also create havoc. The micro-blogging service Twitter experienced a massive hockey-stick adoption curve that quickly outstripped the capacity of its back-end infrastructure. This resulted in downtimes that frustrated users, especially given that the service is predicated on continuous, instant updates on the question "What are you doing, right now?"

In some ways, Twitter is an example of a company doing the right things when building out a speculative new product to deal with an X-problem. It started almost as a whimsical experiment, and the development team used off-the-shelf technology and products wherever possible, thus reducing the investment and development time. After launch, the standardized technology—with its standardized interfaces—also made it easy for others to write add-on functionality for Twitter, which helped its popularity.

But Twitter's rapid rise in popularity meant that the nonoptimized components quickly became a hindrance. According to the company's Web site, in 2007 and 2008 Twitter's uptime was around 98 percent. This sounds quite good, but what if your telephone didn't work for a week out of the year? That's what 2 percent downtime means, and Twitter's value proposition is immediacy, so users see any downtime as very unsatisfactory.

By early 2007, a little over a year after the company started, user complaints had reached a crescendo. Being a modern communication company, Twitter was in constant conversation with its users. Many of the users were very publicly throwing around ideas for how Twitter's technology could be improved, an easy thing for them to do since many of Twitter's users were programmers making other Web 2.0 kinds of services. This prompted Alex Payne, one of the programmers at Twitter, to post on the company's blog in May 2008:

> Twitter is, fundamentally, a messaging system. Twitter was not
> architected as a messaging system, however. For expediency's sake,
> Twitter was built with technologies and practices that are more

appropriate to a content management system. Over the last year and a half we've tried to make our system behave like a messaging system as much as possible, but that's introduced a great deal of complexity and unpredictability.... Our direction going forward is to replace our existing system, component-by-component, with parts that are designed from the ground up to meet the requirements that have emerged as Twitter has grown.[13]

This forced the team to rebuild the system piece by piece while Twitter was still up and running. Because it is a live service, they could not easily take it down, swap pieces out and experiment with them, and then start it back up again, as is possible with conventional software that gets distributed in distinct releases. They had to change the tires—and the engine and the chassis—while the car was hurtling down the highway at ever-increasing speed. Furthermore, they had to make all these changes to the internals without breaking any of the complementary add-ons made by external developers.

No one has a crystal ball when it comes to anticipating actual customer demand. It is necessary to make some informed judgments (based on thorough immersion and ongoing feedback) about the likelihood of different customer adoption scenarios, future needs, and the relative complexity and cost of building those in the future or putting in standardized interfaces to allow them later.

Integrated Roadmap Planning

Because rapid systeming requires coordinated evolution of the entire ecosystem, touchpoints, and other related elements, well-planned and communicated roadmaps are essential. At frog it is common for us to deliver roadmaps to clients that startle them with their breadth: physical products, embedded interfaces, Web site design, PC applications, mobile applications, value propositions, underlying software and Web technologies, brand attributes, product tiers and lines, staffing, partner initiatives, retail channel changes, and the dependencies among all of these.

This does not mean roadmaps need to run far out into the future. Quite the contrary, since you are working under the assumption that you do not fully know the problem you are trying to solve and are using the rapid systeming approach to create solutions to help uncover the problem, you should not fool yourself by overdetailing a foggy future. Your emphasis should be on near-term close coordination across the relevant system components and participants, coupled with a high-level long-term vision that provides the boundaries of what to focus on and what to ignore.

Juggling Clockspeeds

Coordinating roadmaps across companies (or across business units for that matter) implies aligning the clockspeeds that each works at. The term *clockspeed*, popularized by Charles Fine in his book of the same name, denotes the speed at which a company or category goes through generational cycles of technologies and new product launches.[14] Pity the poor automotive manufacturers tackling the X-problem of how to handle an ever-widening landscape of media and data connectivity in the car when their clockspeeds are four to six years, and the digital technologies they are integrating are operating on six- to twelve-month clockspeeds.

Most ecosystems do not have such large disparities. Nevertheless, clockspeeds need to be taken into account when creating roadmaps that lay out generational shifts and dependencies in the ecosystem.

Rapid systeming will stress the development organization in ways that it is not used to. If done inefficiently, the iterative pace and flexibility will drop off dramatically. The economic value of the system will diminish quickly for everyone facing too-frequent iterations that are costly to achieve (perhaps due to poorly designed interfaces or too much customization required each time), and that affect large numbers of linkages between system components.[15]

A flexible system that can adapt rapidly is worthless if it lacks direction on what to adapt to and how to adapt. The system must be kept up to date on emerging changes in the surrounding context in order to deliver long-term value and success. Anyone can get lucky with a one-off hit, but sustaining success requires vigilant attention to the gaps between where you are today, where you want to go in the future, and the surrounding contextual realities.

The Motorola Razr and the Missing Feedback Loop

The Motorola Razr, launched in 2004, became one of the best-selling mobile phones of all time. But it was considered anything but a sure bet inside Motorola. Geoffrey Frost, the CMO who oversaw its development, had to fend off skepticism in the hidebound Motorola organization. "Our traditional research told us that there was a total available world market of about two million units for a $499 phone," said Frost. The last genuine hit that Motorola had was the StarTac phone in 1996. The Razr was intended to restore the luster to the brand by being a high-status, low-volume, money-losing product.[16]

The Razr was only an average phone by most traditional measures. Its camera was poor quality, the user interface was frequently criticized as hard to use, the battery life was unexceptional. But the phone's sleek metal body was half as thick as anything out there, and the edgy form appealed equally to men and women (putting a lie to the stereotype that women only want soft, rounded products; in fact the Razr's sister product, Pebl, was meant to be feminine-looking — and it was a flop compared to the Razr).[17]

Despite its drawbacks, the Razr's unique attributes caused it to blow past all projections, selling not two million units worldwide, but two million in the U.K. alone. "So the real lesson is," Frost observed, "the best way to predict the future, as Peter Drucker once said, is to create it. The best way to predict the total available market for a new thing is to invent it." And I love what he says next: "If you want to be a leading company, you have to create the products that create your destiny."[18]

Sadly, Frost passed away soon after the Razr's launch, and Motorola was not able to sustain the momentum that the Razr created. Frost's knack for spotting a breakthrough product was not possessed by the rest of the organization. Follow-on products were either too incremental or too flawed. Competitors that were already superior to the first Razr on specifications like camera and battery caught up to its thinness within a year or two, and mimicked its styling and use of metal. The style qualities that allowed the Razr to capitalize on the shift from cell phones being utilitarian gadgets to fashion accessories were now neutralized. Motorola failed to keep up with the changing tide and the improving competition, and just two years after the Razr reset the rules of the category, Motorola had lost its best-selling status to LG and Samsung.

Feedback Loops

The present should be a beta of the future we want to live in.
—Fabio Sergio

What starts out as delightful becomes expected, and the expected becomes banal. It took many years for electric windows to change from being luxury items (as my grandfather experienced in his Renault test drive) to standard features on even the least expensive cars. But today's demanding customers expect that shift to happen much more quickly. Tracking the ever-changing gap between expectations and actual offerings on the market is crucial in dynamic categories. Companies must establish robust feedback loops to monitor the gap, or risk becoming detached from customer needs. Lack of a feedback loop can also lead a company to rest on its laurels and get unexpectedly disrupted by competitors. Motorola learned this lesson the hard way after the initial success of its Razr mobile phone.[19]

Many of the tools described in Chapter Three, on immersion for X-problem discovery, work equally well for filling a feedback loop with input after product launch:

Ethnography, journals, usability testing: Meet with people using the product and see how well it is working for them, what new needs arise, and how their behaviors have changed as a result of having it. (Some of these could be the same people you visited earlier, so you have a baseline.)

Surveys and focus groups: Continue to conduct these periodically to get updates on perceptions and trends. But still be careful not to limit the scope of the questions prematurely, artificially confirming initial hypotheses while missing out on other opportunities. Because the scope of the X-problem takes time to stabilize, it is easy to close off new opportunities by making assumptions about aspects of it that seem fixed. Carrying such assumptions into surveys and focus groups will tend to harden them into common knowledge that later gets disrupted. To avoid such surprises, stay open-ended longer than you are used to for mature categories.

Customer collaboration: Find the most vocal customers and talk to them. Take advantage of Web-enabled two-way conversation methods like forums and blogs (preferably including your own) to get firsthand feedback. Even if you make physical products that have no online integration, forums are a great way of getting input from your most demanding customers. Use these channels to invite customers for sneak peeks of new concepts and solicit input about unmet needs.[20]

Brand perceptions: How are customers seeing your brand differently since the launch? Are perceptions moving in the desired direction?

Retail: Spend time with customers shopping for your product (and competitors') and sales staff who sell it. See how initial reactions change over time as the novelty wears off, and what kinds of expectations and stated needs customers have walking in the door. Listen to how sales staff diagnose customer needs now compared to before the launch, and how they pitch and position your product against competitors (and your previous products, if applicable).

Tracking the Emerging Competitive Landscape

Motorola lost touch with a fast-moving market and rested on its laurels.

One man who could never be accused of resting on his laurels is Frank Lloyd Wright. Some of his most famous buildings—the Johnson Wax building, Falling Water—were built in a burst of renewed inspiration in his seventies. One of his biggest projects, the Marin County Civic Center, north of San Francisco in San Rafael, California, was built just two years before his death at age ninety-one. It is an architectural beauty, a long, low building tucked in a wooded valley off a highway, its tan stucco exterior glowing in the afternoon sun and contrasting with the sky-blue copper roof. A spire is placed at the center of the roof, and the building's side walls are a series of arches of various sizes, almost like a church cloister.

Autodesk's headquarters are within sight of this masterpiece, fittingly enough since it is the leading maker of software for architects, engineers, and designers. Best known for AutoCAD, software that has been a mainstay of building design for decades, Autodesk now has a diverse range of applications for many different yet related industries: landscape design and city planning, animation and sound design for film, product design and engineering, tool design for manufacturing, mapping, and civil engineering.

CEO Carl Bass has a relatively sanguine view of innovation, believing that it is often confused with *invention*. He believes that too often products and technologies are invented without a real sense of how they can be converted into products that people will want to buy and use. This is what marks the transition of an invention into an innovation—recognized market value. Bass argues that large companies such as his are better at applying innovations across product lines, and at the necessary support functions like marketing, distribution, customer service, and sustaining development. Small companies are typically better at up-front invention, but may struggle with the conversion from invention to marketable innovation. He sees no shame in acquiring inventions from the outside once they have had a chance to prove their worth. Like Logitech, Autodesk keeps a sharp eye out for interesting small companies that are early in the S-curve, and whose products will allow Autodesk to complement its existing products and address existing customers in new ways, or reach out to new customers.

Autodesk relies heavily on its 1,900 channel partners and 3,300 development partners to pick up on emerging trends and new ways that customers are trying to use its software. In some cases these partners will fill the needs themselves with customized adaptations of Autodesk's core offerings, but if the need is strong and complex enough, Autodesk itself will spin up development or seek an emerging company tackling that need directly. VP Brian Mathews sees these partners as scouts, looking at the periphery of the business for new opportunities.

Partners such as these can be among the best assets for a company seeking divergence, or one concerned about competitive threats at the edges. Maintaining constant communication, strong relationships, and providing guidelines and perhaps even training on how to spot shifts in the market and dissect customers' changing needs are all vital to making good use of potential scouts.

Scanning the Competitive Periphery

Many of the immersion tools can be used for tracking the changing competitive environment after the product is released.

Toolbox competitors: How do other companies with similar toolboxes to your own respond? Do they recognize the opportunity your product is going after, and extend their toolboxes in similar ways? Are companies lower down in your supply chain angling to move upward and overlap with your position?

Needs-based competitors: How do other competitors who satisfy similar needs react (whether they are direct or indirect competitors) after your product launch? Do they change their positioning or messaging? What new products do they launch in response? How do they change their ecosystems or bring on new partners to counter your launch? Are new competitors (whether established companies or start-ups) popping up, recognizing the opportunity that you have hinted at with the product launch? How are they addressing it in a different way, perhaps seeing things that you missed?

Complementers: Are they jumping on the needs and insights you have uncovered? If so, they may see promise as well, confirming the opportunity but building on it in different directions. Are they exploiting the ecosystem in novel ways by treating it as a platform to build on?

Continue trying out the new competitive and complementary products as you did during development, to get a feel for the experiences they deliver. Talk with makers of complementary products and with others in your direct ecosystem, as Autodesk does, and use their peripheral vision to extend your own, casting as wide a net as possible over the emerging competitive landscape.

As the X-problem emerges and your understanding matures based on immersion and customer feedback, you face a big question: how much do you trust your immersion findings and instincts about your vision for the future, and how much do you pay attention to skeptical customers who may be experts on *today* but have a limited perspective on the future?

Salesforce.com — Success by Ignoring Customers

One company that stuck to its guns is Salesforce.com, which makes Web-based customer relationship management (CRM) software. Salesforce is a pioneer in Software as a Service, or SaaS: offering applications by subscription through a Web browser rather than as installed individually on each PC. Marc Benioff left Oracle to start Salesforce, and he had a vision to shift CRM over to a SaaS approach.

SaaS would mean that all of a customer's precious — and secret — sales and client contact data would now be hosted on Salesforce's own servers rather than inside the customer's firewall. It's the difference between using an e-mail application like Outlook, and using Gmail — one is kept locally, the other hosted remotely in the cloud. This caused, to say the least, a lot of skepticism among potential customers. Clarence So, an early employee of Salesforce and now its VP of community, recalls, "People were saying, 'This stuff will never fly. Companies will never let anyone host their data.' The word *control* came up a lot."

Investors pushed Salesforce to offer a traditional solution as well as the SaaS version. Benioff didn't buy it. "We were going to go whole hog into the hosted model," Clarence So says. "Marc felt that the control issue was just an emotional issue, not really a rational issue." (Call it an example of an experience need masquerading as a functional need.)

Salesforce had two core insights that caused it to ignore what its potential customers were saying they wanted:

- In an increasingly mobile and data-distributed world, the value of a Web-based approach would come to outweigh centralized storage and control.
- Small and medium-sized businesses could not afford the usual high-end products, and the reduced costs and maintenance headaches of SaaS would particularly appeal to them.

It took several years, but it turned out that Benioff's insights were correct, and the customers (and the common wisdom) were wrong. Many of those same skeptical customers are now subscribers to Salesforce. The company has been rewarded with around 50 percent year-on-year revenue growth for several years, and an increase from 400,000 subscribers in 2006 to over a million just two years later. And its traditional CRM competitors like Oracle and SAP are all considering SaaS offerings of their own.[21]

Stay True to Vision, or Change with Feedback?

> *Don't worry about other people stealing your ideas. If your ideas are any good you'll have to ram them down people's throats.*
> —HOWARD AIKENS, IBM ENGINEER

The Salesforce story is a perfect example of the phenomenon Howard Aikens is ruefully describing. We have all seen an intriguing new idea shot down prematurely. New ideas are inevitably rough, full of holes, unproven. The more radical the idea, the more this will be true. If an organization is set up for incremental innovation, the bias will be to poke the holes rather than support the promise. Often a charismatic and influential leader is necessary to shepherd the ideas along and provide the high-level guiding vision, as Benioff and Frost did.

But the best leaders recognize that sticking to a vision come hell or high water can also be a recipe for disaster. In the face of rapid change, effective adaption requires an understanding of the gap between how the world is and your aspirations for how it could be. But it can often be hard to bridge that gap conceptually.

To quote another sage, St. Hubbins (that would be David St. Hubbins, of the fictional heavy metal band Spinal Tap), "It's such a fine line between stupid and clever." This sums up the paradox. How do you deal with the fact that sometimes clever and stupid are the exact same thing, and it is just a matter of timing that determines whether you are a hero or a zero?

FIGURE 6.3 Vision Versus Test.

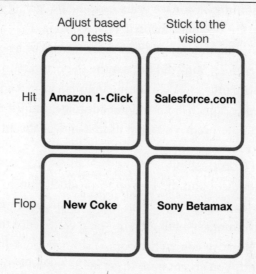

So is it better to adhere closely to your vision, or to adapt the concept based on feedback from experts and customers, and changes in the competitive context? Figure 6.3 illustrates the capriciousness of this dilemma, with these well-known examples showing that both staying true to the vision and adjusting it can result in hits or flops.

As described earlier, Jeff Bezos's vision for 1-Click met initial resistance from customers when tested. Nonetheless, by making some small changes Amazon.com turned it into a very popular feature.

By contrast, New Coke, one of the most famous flops in business history, was chasing a need that did not exist—Coca-Cola was simply responding to the taste tests that Pepsi was running on television. The "Pepsi Challenge" commercials showed a flavor test where people on the street were asked to compare samples of Pepsi and Coca-Cola, with Pepsi unsurprisingly coming out on top.[22] Coca-Cola changed its formula to match the comparatively sweeter Pepsi, and New Coke was born. But New Coke was a knee-jerk response and was not truly rooted in what customers wanted.

Like New Coke, Betamax has become a synonym for product failure, albeit one that hung on for ten years or so before giving up the ghost. Sony's vision for Betamax focused on recording TV shows, but its one-hour recording time was too short for movies or lengthy sporting events. Furthermore, Sony did not see the opportunity in selling tapes prerecorded with movies. JVC's competing VHS format addressed both these issues. After launch, Sony did not adequately adjust to respond to emergent customer needs, costing it its first-mover advantage.

Passion and Compassion

During development and the run-up to product launch, you want to be looking at the emerging problem definition from as many angles as possible to give yourself a full picture—and confidence that the vision is on target. Negative comments from customers must be put in that broader context. You do not want to get in the trap of letting customers lead you around by the nose. As my colleague Albert Tan observes, focus groups were originally called that because they were intended to *focus* the research; they were never intended to *be* the research. Unfortunately, at many organizations, focus groups have become a substitute for taking ownership of the vision, as was the case at Coca-Cola.

Sadly, there is no pat answer whether to stay unwavering to your vision or adjust it based on feedback.

Another frog colleague, Mark Olson, suggests a nice way to think about it. First, do you have *passion* for the vision? Are you truly committed to it because you believe in its potential? Do you see promise where naysayers only see faults? Do you see the cleverness where others see stupidity? Second, is the vision rooted in *compassion* for customers? In other words, is it based on a deep understanding of underlying customer needs, perhaps ones that they have not expressed explicitly?

If both of these are true, then staying close to the vision may well be the correct course. If only one or the other is true, then you should stay open to new possibilities for what the vision is, or what customers truly need.

High Panic Threshold

A way to evaluate your passion and compassion for an innovation is to think about your panic threshold. In other words, how much patience will you have to ride out the early ambiguity and rapid flux before calling it a day?

Wayne Gretsky, the ice hockey great, was a patient man. He was said to have the highest panic threshold of any player. Other players would panic and strike too early, but he had the nerve to wait until just the right moment to shoot, watching where other players were on the ice and looking for the opening. Similarly, it takes discipline and nerve to wait out adaption and not prematurely lock down the definition of the X-problem or what your approach to it will be. Doing so risks missing out on the real opportunity.

Collecting $200 million would seem like a good opportunity, yet Google passed it up. Why? Marissa Mayer, Google's VP of search product and user experience, has said that Google could make that much in a year by putting ads on results from its Image Search product, but chose not to. They felt that it would not be worth the predicted drop in usage of the product (about 1 percent).[23] This is an example of Google's long-term thinking, its high panic threshold.

Bala Iyer and Thomas Davenport refer to this as Google's "strategic patience" and cite it as a key lesson for any company looking to do innovation seriously. They argue that with its farsighted mission to organize all the world's information and make it accessible, "the short-term profitability of a new offering doesn't seem to matter as much to Google as it might to other businesses. CEO Eric Schmidt has estimated that it will take 300 years to achieve the mission of organizing the world's information. His 1,200-quarter forecast might invite smirking; still, it illustrates Google's long-term approach to building value and capability."[24]

Google is in a luxurious position: its search advertising business has made it extremely profitable. But even that was anything but inevitable.

When Google first appeared, search functionality was considered a commodity, a simple cost-of-entry feature for a Web portal. As late as 2001—some three years after its founding—Google had no idea how it was going to make money. "We really couldn't figure out the business model," recalls Michael Moritz, an investor in the firm while at Sequoia Capital. "There was a period where things were looking pretty bleak. We were burning cash, and the enterprise [search market] was rejecting us." It was only after several iterations of search-based advertising, and observing how other companies, such as Overture, Yahoo, and the now-forgotten GoTo.com, were innovating that Google hit on its golden goose: AdWords, its method of making specific ads appear on search results pages based on keywords selected by the advertiser.[25]

X-problems can put you in a prolonged state of ambiguity as the opportunities, possible solutions, and innovations gradually reveal themselves. This can test the patience of any executive.

If You Panic, Learn from It

Sometimes it takes panicking and acting against better judgment to make an organization reaffirm its values and goals. This clarifies its long-term focus, helping make better near-term decisions. One company that lived through that lesson is Clif Bar, a maker of energy snacks.

The idea for the original Clif Bars came about when founder Gary Erickson was on a long bike ride, for which he'd stocked up on PowerBars, the original energy snack for athletes. Put off by their bland taste and unpleasant texture, he reached a point when he couldn't stomach another one. He stopped at a convenience store and wolfed down some powdered donuts instead. And then he set about creating a better-tasting energy snack.[26]

Since its original product in 1992, Clif has expanded its range beyond sports and into healthy "lifestyle" and kids' snacks, and the company has grown by 50 percent almost every year.

Like its competitors, the company got caught up in the low-carb Atkins diet fad of the early 2000s. Clif resisted it, Erickson recalls, "But the Atkins diet had turned the whole food industry upside down for a period of about a year and a half. All our retailers and distributors were telling us to come out with a low-carb product. . . . We didn't want to do it, but we did. And it was a me-too product, with ingredients whose names you can't pronounce and that I'm embarrassed to say we put in there. We lost about a million dollars—not only was the product not good, but by the time it came out the low-carb craze was over."

Clif Bar had panicked, choosing to chase a short-term opportunity at the expense of its original vision. "That shook us up, and we learned from it," says Erickson. "It got us back to our roots. And this is the reason we are still competitive: we are true to who we are, authentic to our story and our products."[27]

Strategy

X-problems present companies and their leadership with some challenging strategic questions: How to define what the company is about and where to focus? How to understand needs of demanding customers and stay ahead of sophisticated and unexpected competitors? How to prioritize innovation efforts? And ultimately, how to decide what to make that will create revenue by answering these questions?

There is no single right answer. What worked well yesterday may not work well today and in the future. In the preceding chapters I laid out some approaches, tools, frameworks, and examples that I hope provide a sense of a way forward, and that allow the dissection of an X-problem into more manageable sub-problems.

Running through all these methods are challenges that will affect how you approach immersion, convergence, and divergence:

- *Managing an innovation portfolio* and assessing relative risks and investment levels of innovation ideas
- *Working with ecosystem partners* to solve the X-problem and deploy solutions
- *Identifying high-priority ecosystem investments* that will provide long-term advantage and open up market opportunities
- *Dealing with commoditization of categories* as products improve to meet customer expectations

Managing an Innovation Portfolio

Given the increasingly near-term demands of quarterly stock prices and the ever-shortening tenures of executives (often under five years for CEOs and less than two for CMOs),[1] it is no surprise that many companies have biased their innovation efforts toward near-term quick hits. One study showed that over a fourteen-year period from 1990 to 2004, the number of new-to-world innovations introduced each year declined by over 40 percent, new-to-company by over 30 percent, while at the same time improvements and modifications to existing products rose by 80 percent.[2] As a result, many companies' innovation portfolios look like the one in Figure 7.1, with a sharp drop-off of longer-term innovation investments.

Even though they have lower risk and are quicker to bring to market, incremental innovations usually have less possibility of sustained competitive advantage. A near-term focus can also get companies trapped in a cycle of chasing trends rather than creating trends for others

FIGURE 7.1 Innovation Portfolio.

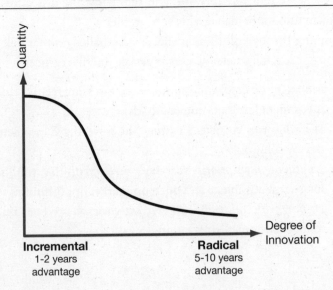

to follow. Remember Motorola's Geoffrey Frost's words: "If you want to be a leading company, you have to create the products that create your destiny."

Too many companies still treat small experimental initiatives at the periphery of the business as riskier than big, expensive initiatives focused on the core business.

Gary Hamel argues, "It is perverse that in many companies billion dollar commitments to moribund businesses can be thought of as 'safe,' while Lilliputian experiments are viewed as risky. Risk is the product of investment multiplied by the probability of failure. A $100,000 experiment with an 80 percent chance of failing is substantially less risky than a $100 million investment with a 1 percent chance of failure.... Yet which would be quicker to win funding in your company? Most companies fail to grasp this simple arithmetic. In the end, though, companies don't need more risk takers; they need people who understand how to de-risk big aspirations."[3]

Clif Bar takes a portfolio approach to innovations to provide stability along with flexibility to explore riskier new areas. It has many near-term incremental products in the pipeline, and balances these with more speculative ideas that emerge through experimentation. Because it is so close to its customers, the company tends to have a good sense of when an idea is going to be mainstream and when it will be a more niche product, and it gauges efforts and expectations accordingly. The company invests proportionately in new ideas, putting in only as much as necessary to keep them moving along. If an idea does not pan out, relatively little has been invested.

Following this approach the company has created a solid product line, very few duds (like the too-late Atkins bar), and some big successes. Not every product needs to be a hit, but Clif is also aware that small experiments can sometimes yield unexpectedly big results.

For example, in the late 1990s women started telling Clif that they wanted a lower-calorie snack bar with vitamins and nutrients geared toward women's bodies. Gary Erickson hit the kitchen, being the sole member of the R&D staff at the time, and started working on what would become the Luna Bar.

Clif's expectations for the Luna Bar were modest. It knew from the customer input that there was latent demand, but as with all its product introductions it hoped for the best but planned for modest success. In fact, Luna outstripped Clif's wildest dreams once it hit the market in April 1999. "We had projected a million and a half in sales," explains Erickson, "and it did 10 million. We had orders for 12 million, but we couldn't fill them as our contract baker was maxed out. The next year it went to 29 million and just kept going. It was a grand slam, the right product at the right time."

What also surprised Erickson was that Luna's smaller size and sweeter taste were a hit with men as well as with women. Not only did Clif address an unmet need for women; it stumbled onto a male market it had not even expected.[4]

Practice Wasteful Innovation

Most organizations are understandably concerned about efficiency—getting the most value out of any effort. Spending resources on lots of small higher-risk experiments can seem wasteful, especially if they are going after ambiguous problems. Such organizations need to rethink the notion of what *waste* means.

Each fall, thousands of people flock to tour a garbage dump. They drive through it admiringly, and take walks to soak in its beauty. Children play in it, and joyfully kick up the garbage. In fact, this part of the world is famous for its dumping of garbage.

I'm talking not about a landfill but about the state of Vermont, where the maple, birch, and beech trees shed their golden and rust colored leaves for the winter. But of course there is no landfill for the leaves in Vermont, or anywhere else for that matter. Nature does not need landfills, despite the vast amounts of what could be called waste that it creates in order to ensure, in aggregate, the survival of the species.

So be like Mother Nature and practice *wasteful* innovation. That may sound crazy, but only if you see waste as a dead end.

In nature, waste equals food (as architect and sustainability expert William McDonaugh tidily puts it). Natural waste always becomes nutrition for something else and gets reborn as a new organism. Waste is just fine if it is cheap to produce and can easily be converted into new resources and new life.[5]

It's best to take a similar view of experiments in your innovation portfolio. In fact it is vital to do so, since failure is guaranteed at some point when innovating. Failed innovations are just fine if you invested in them appropriately and can learn from them to do better next time, or can recycle them for use in another way.

Failed concepts can become food for future efforts in several different ways:

- *Put the concept into the organizational toolbox* for use by others in a different context, or at a different time. Remember, it's a fine line between stupid and clever, often it's just a matter of timing or circumstance. Nonsticky adhesive, like that found on Post-it notes, does not make sense in most situations, but for small pieces of paper that you want to move around, it's perfect.
- *Incorporate the failure as an element in another concept,* rather than keeping it a stand-alone concept. Although not strong enough to stand on its own, it could be a valuable supporting player.
- *Recognize how the failure eliminates possibilities.* The team now has a better understanding of what does *not* work, which helps narrow the possibilities for what *will* work. The failure may have uncovered some heretofore-unseen aspect of customer perceptions, for example, that can guide future development.
- *Abstract up a layer from the failure.* If this particular incarnation did not work, is there something valuable in the principle behind the concept? Often I hear "we tried that already, and it didn't work" when the failure was one of implementation, but the underlying concept was sound.

Plant Seeds, Not Forests

Implicit in the notion of wasteful innovation is that you want to be able to experiment cheaply and without catastrophe, spreading risk across your portfolio. You don't want to have to go to full market launch before finding out the product is a flop.

I once attended a lecture by musician Brian Eno (*Music for Airports,* producer for *The Talking Heads*) and video game creator Will Wright (inventor of *The Sims* and *Spore*). At first it wasn't apparent what they had in common, but soon the connecting thread emerged: both worked with simple modules (musical phrases, game characters) and then set them in motion governed by simple rules. From such humble beginnings would spring wonderfully complex music and games.

Eno summed it up with the phrase, "Plant seeds, not forests." This stuck with me as a way of thinking about approaching innovation in an X-problem world.

Seeds are light on resources to create, can be spread around easily, and through their growth provide feedback about fertile new areas. If an individual seed fails to grow and bear fruit, it's not a tragic loss—it's just one of many that had a chance to succeed. Seeds are a way of reducing risk for big aspirations by spreading the risk around.

Some companies take the seed notion to heart. Google pursues hundreds of projects simultaneously, which it gradually whittles down to a Top 100 list.[6] Google is famous for keeping products in "perpetual beta," with almost half its products in beta at any one time. Some argue that Google has redefined the notion of beta entirely. No longer is it a short temporary phase prior to the "real" product; beta in Google's mind is a long period of adaption, intended to discover the true nature of the problem and thereby optimize the solution.[7]

The Seed Spectrum

Another profligate seed-spreader is Capital One, the credit card company, which does an astonishing twenty thousand experiments per year. Many of these are very small—changing the color of the envelope a new offer is sent in, for example, to see how it affects response rate—while others are larger experiments, such as trials of new interest rates or types of offers.[8]

You should similarly take advantage of the broad array of sizes of seeds that are available to try out innovations at all stages of development. Each seed type has its own pros and cons in terms of development costs and times, and risk level (how much invested versus how much insight returned). In rough order of increasing cost, development intensity, and riskiness, innovation seeds include:

- Illustration
- Spreadsheet
- Paper prototype
- Physical model or prototype
- On-screen prototype
- Concept video
- Partial market test
- Fast-follower

Illustration

An illustration is a simple drawing showing the concept—super cheap, disposable, and easy to change. In the right hands, an illustration can elicit a lot of valuable feedback and be used as a platform on which to conceptualize new behaviors with customers, colleagues, or partners. Illustrating the product is one approach, but illustrations can also be storyboards showing usage scenarios step-by-step, ecosystem maps, napkin sketches, computer renderings, collaborative whiteboard sessions, or any other visual depiction that communicates the idea.

Spreadsheet

A spreadsheet is a prototype, and should be iterated in step with the emerging concept to ensure that the business case and product are aligned. Michael Schrage of MIT's Sloan School of Business describes spreadsheets as a "shared space" that provides a forum "where ideas are created and their practical value is debated.... The spreadsheet projections present a portrait of a predicted future. Spreadsheets can speak louder than words."[9]

Paper Prototype

For evaluating software and interactions, a common approach is *paper prototyping,* where each screen is quickly drawn on a separate sheet of paper, and the screens are then stacked up. One testing technique is to stack sheets of paper with a clip at the top so that they flip like an animation, and place them on a physical stand to mimic the actual screen. Users can then try out the sequence of screens and give feedback on the flow. Very cheap, yet effective.

Physical Model or Prototype

A model (an object that looks like the real thing) or prototype (one that works like the real thing but may not look exactly like it) is invaluable for feedback that cannot be gathered through drawings. These objects can be almost anything that gives insight into physical form and function, whether of the whole product or just a small part of it. Prototypes of physical products can run the gamut from cardboard to machined metal. James Dyson, inventor of the Dyson bag-less cyclone vacuum cleaner, famously says that he created more than five thousand prototypes in five years of development. That equates to four prototypes every weekday, so obviously not all of those were totally new prototypes built from the ground up or full-blown working vacuum cleaners (especially since he was working solo for much of the time).[10]

On-Screen Prototype

For evaluating software and screen-based devices, on-screen prototypes can be either "click-through" demos (where one screen leads inexorably to the next, like a PowerPoint presentation), or more sophisticated interactive demos where the user chooses the path. The latter are more realistic—but more time-consuming to develop. These can either be done as simulations or as actual prototypes, in which case real code is used. For IPC, the frog team used screen simulations on a laptop to supplement the paper and physical prototypes, again avoiding the complexity of trying to get the screens to work in an actual unit. This gave the team the freedom to experiment quickly and continuously, decoupling volatility of the hardware and software from each other.

Concept Video

A concept video is a narrative video that illustrates usage scenarios and the value proposition. This can be an effective tool for communicating with potential customers to get a first impression, or to generate excitement within an organization or with ecosystem partners.

Partial Market Test

You can do a limited production run and test in a small population. This is frequently done as *bucket testing* with Web sites, where users are randomly presented new designs for pages without prior notice, and their behaviors tracked and compared to users who act as control samples. For physical products this random approach is not possible, but small market entries can be used as a way of getting highly accurate (though relatively costly) information back about customer behaviors and perceptions.

Fast-Follower

As with Autodesk and Logitech, the fast-follower approach can be a successful method of growth, whether through internal innovation or through acquisition. But it has its own risks. You must be confident in your ability to spot categories at the bottom of their S-curves, and be comfortable integrating a new acquisition into the larger organization. The costs of this seed type can vary dramatically, but the risks are relatively low since the concept has been proven in the near term (though whether it will continue to have legs is another matter).

Using Seeds

Seeds should be treated as catalysts for conversation, not just evaluated on a pass/fail basis. They are ways for the team to ask itself, "Is this what we wanted?" just as each release of a product out into the world asks customers, "How is this working for you?" Any given prototype will succeed at some things and do less well at others, but in either case you will have gained further insight into how to solve the X-problem.

Schrage argues, "The value of prototypes resides less in the models themselves than in the interactions—the conversations, arguments, consultations, collaborations—they invite. Prototypes force individuals and institutions to confront the tyranny of trade-offs. That confrontation, in turn, forces people to play seriously with the difficult choices they must ultimately make. The fundamental question isn't, 'What kinds of models, prototypes and simulations should we be building?' but 'What kind of interactions do we want to create?'"[11]

One important lesson that we have learned at frog from working with clients is that the early concept representations need to get outside the immediate product team. Tangible models and prototypes are instrumental to creating buy-in at multiple levels of the organization. They engage people rationally (What does it do? Does it work?) and emotionally, with the kick that comes from seeing something tangible for the first time.

As Schrage says, "It's far easier for clients [or managers] to articulate what they want by playing with prototypes than by enumerating requirements. People don't order ingredients from a menu; they order meals. The quick-and-dirty prototype is a medium of co-development with the client [or management]."[12]

Prototypes should be *charismatic,* he says. "In world-class companies, an interesting prototype emits the social and intellectual equivalent of a magnetic field, attracting smart people with interesting ideas about how to make it better."[13] On the other hand, prototypes that fail to attract attention may be a sign that people do not have much interest in the underlying idea. At Google, the number of people interested in a particular project is one of the criteria used to decide whether to continue funding it. If Google's own staff is not demonstrating enthusiasm, how can the company expect customers to be?[14]

Finding Seeds in the Outside World

Companies have increasingly been turning to outsiders to expand the breadth of their innovation portfolios, using arrangements that are more creative than simple make/buy decisions. The open innovation model popularized by Henry Chesbrough has gained significant traction at companies like Procter & Gamble, who use smart brains outside the company to supplement their own. While the crowdsourcing approach using online forums is an example of customer collaboration, open innovation focuses on collaboration among ecosystem and value chain partners, along with other outside companies seeking to connect for development and distribution reach. Indeed, when dealing with ecosystem-level problems, it will be necessary to bring any other partners in the ecosystem along and collaborate in solving the X-problem.[15]

Innovation through acquisition is not unusual, especially in software. Apple, Microsoft, Google, and Yahoo are all examples of large software companies that have achieved some or most of their expansion through acquisitions, buying innovative software capabilities rather than building a particular innovation internally. Yes, even Google—by the end of 2008 it had acquired fifty-four other companies, including ones that underpin some of its major strategic products: YouTube, DoubleClick, Blogger, JotSpot, Android, Picasa, and Keyhole (which became Google Earth).

Sustainability is also an area where established companies often go the acquisition route, such as Clorox buying Burt's Bees (skin care products), and Colgate-Palmolive acquiring Tom's of Maine (dental care). As green products become mainstream, established companies are quietly acquiring pioneering brands in order to benefit from the imminent growth. The larger companies benefit from the knowledge gained with the seed company, and the acquired company gains in development, distribution, and marketing resources.

Looking to the outside for innovations has clearly worked well for some. But it does have its risks and is not universally applicable.

Bill Buxton, a researcher at Microsoft and author of the book *Sketching User Experiences*, argues that relying almost entirely on external sources of innovation is risky and limiting. "What happens when there is no company or technology to buy, license or merge with? What do you do when the company is there, but you do not have the skills or the resources to do a deal?"[16] A total focus on innovation through acquisition can become a crutch that saps a company's ability to do innovation internally when it must. Innovation efforts need to go along at a certain clip, to have a critical mass if you will, to be self-sustaining. Otherwise the company gets rusty and out of practice. It's a muscle that needs to be continually worked out or it atrophies.

Too often at frog, I've seen companies that have let their innovation muscles go. Their processes, mind-sets, tolerance for risk and ambiguity, and analytical methods have all become focused and attuned for incrementalism and business as usual. When facing disruptions or zipping off the top of their industry S-curve, they are starting at a huge disadvantage. It takes so long to get limbered up and back into shape that the project is mostly over by the time they really hit their stride.

So even if pursuing a heavy course of sourcing innovations from the outside, keep the internal innovation initiatives going. And don't just focus internal innovations on incremental efforts, either; foster riskier initiatives too. You have to keep reminding yourself of what the pain of innovation can feel like, or you lose the tolerance for it.

Working with Ecosystem Partners

X-problems and rapid systeming bring up some strategic issues to consider when collaborating with others. In Chapter Six, I discussed the need for integrated roadmaps and juggling clockspeeds of different companies involved in the system development. There are several other issues to think about:

- *X-problem disclosure:* How much do you tell ecosystem partners about the X-problem you are trying to solve? Obviously there are risks to how much you reveal. But these should be weighed against the risks that come from not having the perspective and effective innovation assistance from partners who can help you solve the problem more quickly. You may reveal layers of information — pertinent customer needs, or knowledge about toolbox capabilities that must be complemented by the rest of the ecosystem — and keep others hidden, such as core insights and the workings of proprietary technology.

- *Partner longevity:* It is common practice for many companies to change vendors year after year in the search for the lowest price. For commodity products in mature markets this may make sense, but when tackling an X-problem's many unknowns, having partners who can build up experience and perspective through several iterations is a big benefit.

- *Mutual benefits:* Over the long term, ecosystems work best if all the participants gain from them, and not just the originator reaps all the rewards. Marco Iansiti and Roy Levien argue that ensuring partner success was part of what helped eBay thrive, and ignoring it contributed to the downfall of Enron. Both were ecosystem hubs, but the strategies they pursued were very different. eBay's auctions helped make others successful, while Enron's electricity trading schemes scraped off most of the profits and left little for the partners (and in reality it was accumulating massive losses that it kept hidden in secret accounts).[17]

Experience Performance and Competitiveness

As a new category of product emerges, the quality of customer experience is typically rather poor. That is to say, its *experience performance* is not yet sufficient to make it appeal beyond early adopters who will put up with its eccentricities because it is filling some pressing need. Improving experience performance to a certain threshold is what is required to tip a product category out of a pioneering niche and into more mainstream adoption. There was not much performance difference between the first- and second-generation Prius; what changed dramatically was the quality of the experience. Early car-sharing programs mostly appealed to hard-core environmentalists who wanted to supplement public transit, but were not convenient enough for a broader audience until services like Zipcar worked out the kinks.

Sometimes the experience suffers because the underlying technology is not good enough, as was the case with early cell phones: they were large and clunky, which limited their appeal only to those who *really* needed to stay in touch all the time. In this case, the products' *functional performance* degraded the experience performance. But experience and functional performance are not necessarily related. Earlier I talked about the way hard drives had exceeded what most people needed from a functional point of view (capacity, speed, reliability), but were still not good enough from an experience perspective.

If one is clever, good experience performance can be delivered in spite of relatively poor functional performance. Nintendo has dominated the video game console market recently with its Wii, beating the combined sales of Sony's Playstation and Microsoft's Xbox. Nintendo outsold these two functionally superior competitors by being ingenious with how it approached experience performance. It took the focus off pure processing and graphics speed, and shifted it to gameplay enjoyment with novel usage interactions like the motion-sensing remote.

Figure 7.2 illustrates several scenarios for how experience and functional performance can relate. Each has differing implications for how to be competitive.

Scenario 1. This is the Early Hybrid Cars scenario, in which neither the functional nor the experience performance of the first-generation hybrids was good enough to appeal to a wide audience. This is a typical situation early in a category's life at the bottom of the S-curve, ripe for innovation and improvement in both technology and experience performance. Depending on a company's capabilities, it may be feasible to improve one aspect ahead of the other, but either one should provide differentiation and wider appeal. Understanding whether customers' unmet needs are primarily functional or experiential will determine the innovation focus.

FIGURE 7.2 Competitiveness Scenarios.

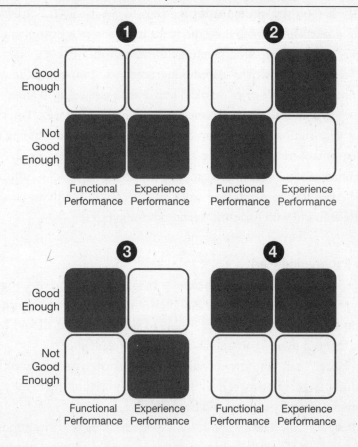

Scenario 2. This is the Razr scenario, where Motorola dramatically improved experience performance but left functional performance lagging. For a while this was OK, but competitors then caught up on experience performance and exceeded Motorola on functional performance. Generally speaking this is a less common scenario, as most attention tends to go to functional performance early in a category's evolution, and it often takes great ingenuity to make a good experience out of a mediocre technology. In this case, customers like using the available products, but technology innovation could enable new behaviors and value propositions that will reset experience expectations.

Scenario 3. This is the Maxtor situation, where functional performance has outstripped functional needs, but experiential needs are going unmet. Improving the experience can open new customers and market opportunities, thus creating differentiation.

Scenario 4. This is a commodity scenario. Two trends tend to dominate here: low-price battles, and ever-lengthening feature lists as competitors seek out temporary incremental advantages. You need to get very good at working in a low-margin business, identifying new dimensions of competition that shift the terms of the debate, or diversify into other product areas. There may be possibilities for niche customers who have extra demands and will pay a premium for them (such as Logitech found with mice and keyboards for gamers).

The Experience Gap

In scenarios one and three, where experience performance is not good enough, there is an *experience gap* between what people want from a product and what the product is able to deliver. A goal should be to close that gap in order to unlock wider mainstream appeal.

Figure 7.3 shows how the customer experience performance in a product category improves over time, gradually catching up to the point where the majority of users will be satisfied.

People's expectations about the experience they get from products tend to go up. They do not start at zero—there is always a minimum bar that must be met (and as I have been arguing, this minimum is itself gradually rising, often influenced by experiences in unrelated categories). Not everyone has the same level of expectations, of course; the line shown in Figure 7.3 is an average. The early adopters will put up with more and have lower expectations, and they allow a new product type to get started. But for a product to break into the mainstream it must improve the experience to the point where it aligns with the expectations of a larger audience.

(I've also shown the line here as a smooth curve. But disruptions can drastically reset expectations upward, such as the iPhone did with

FIGURE 7.3 Experience Gap.

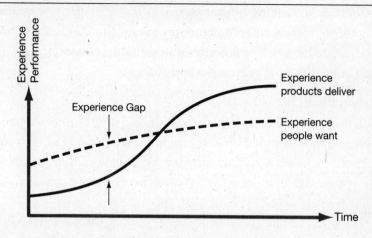

the smartphone category, or Amazon's Kindle did for the e-reader category.)

As experience performance improves and closes the gap, it eventually hits a *crossover* point where it meets, and eventually exceeds, what customers need (Figure 7.4). The crossover signals that unmet experiential needs have been identified and met for an average customer.

FIGURE 7.4 Experience Crossover.

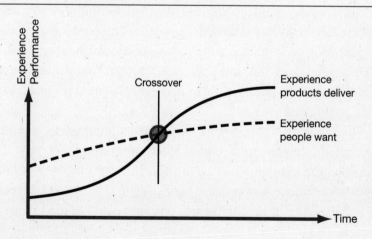

The improved experience at the crossover point is what allows the hockey stick of adoption to take place in the growth stage of the industry S-curve, as the product becomes more appealing to customers beyond niche early adopters. The faster you can get to the crossover point, the better your chances of creating widespread adoption.

Closing the Experience Gap

If you find yourself in scenario one (early hybrid cars) or three (Maxtor), where adoption is stifled because customers are dissatisfied with your products' experience performance and have significant unmet needs, then you need to examine what is causing the experience gap and what it will take to close it.

If the gap can be closed using better convergence of touchpoints, as with Maxtor, then that is a relatively straightforward, low-cost, and rapid path. But do not underestimate the difficulty of doing it well, however; it's no accident that so few companies succeed at creating coherent touchpoint matrices. For that reason, do not dismiss it as a flash-in-the-pan differentiation.

You face more structurally far-reaching choices if your immersion research reveals that closing the experience gap depends on integrating the ecosystem more tightly by taking ownership of a larger footprint.

It is a common pattern in any technology-driven category—the PC is often used as the archetypal example—where early in the category's life, high levels of integration are required to improve functional performance as quickly as possible. Since the components contributing to functional performance are not yet good enough, they must be carefully integrated and tuned to work together. Companies that are good at integration (such as IBM or Apple) are the most profitable early in the category life cycle.

Over time, as the individual components improve, the need for customized integration drops and it becomes possible for people to assemble products that achieve more widely acceptable levels of functional performance from off-the-shelf components. As this happens, the value of the integrators drops, and more profits tend to go to the component makers (such as Microsoft or Intel), or to companies that can efficiently bundle and market stock components (such as Dell or HP).[18]

A similar dynamic is in effect with experience performance, though as noted it does not necessarily happen in lockstep timing with functional performance.

To create a car-sharing experience that would be appealing beyond niche environmentalists, Zipcar had to custom-assemble an ecosystem of components. With both the iPod and iPhone, Apple's integrated approach to systems design allowed its products to create vastly improved experiences that unlocked massive market potential, where earlier products that had wrapped better components in worse experiences had little impact.[19]

Just as the PC is the archetype for functional performance, digital music is the archetype for experience performance, as it was one of the first instances where people recognized the value of such a tightly integrated ecosystem and its concomitant experience benefits leading to mainstream adoption and sustained competitive advantage.

With music it was necessary to create an integrated ecosystem to improve the experience enough that it created appeal beyond college students and computer nerds. This is what Apple accomplished. It is not so well known perhaps that the original iPod actually contained very little that Apple invented from scratch. The hard drive, the device OS, the scroll-wheel, the iTunes application, and the anti-piracy protocol were all developed externally. By masterfully combining these third-party elements and adding enough "special sauce" with the automatic music synchronization between PC and iPod, the simple user interface, and iconic industrial design, Apple created a category killer despite being late to market and with a product costing twice as much as its competition.[20]

Today, some key parts of the digital music system are mature enough to be decoupled and don't need to be custom-developed. This has allowed Amazon to make modest inroads into Apple's dominance by biting off just one piece: downloadable music sales. By entering the digital music sales market at a point where music labels were more open-minded about selling tracks without piracy protection (which makes it harder for customers to move music files from one device to another), Amazon did not have to wrestle with all the complexities that this created a few years before. One can foresee a time in the near future when the whole ecosystem will be standardized, freeing up device makers, software developers, and content providers to all compete against their own kind without competing across categories, as is the case today.

After the crossover, once the recipe for delivering an experience with broad appeal has been identified, the need for tight integration drops off. As with cycles of functional performance, the makers of components and those who can bundle stock components together efficiently then tend to get more of the profits, not the integrators of complex systems.

In deciding whether a modular or integrated approach makes sense for a category, look at how quickly the gap can be closed and how soon after the crossover value will shift from integrators to component providers. If it looks like there will be considerable time until the crossover, or that even after the crossover it will take a prolonged period for modular approaches to replicate the necessary experience performance on a wide scale, then an integrated approach makes more sense and is worth investing in. If the crossover is imminent, or the industry will quickly shift to favoring modularity, then a modular approach is preferable. Even if you will be "prematurely modular" and cause an inferior experience for a short while, in the long run it will serve you better.

Evaluating the Gap and Strategic Timing

The tricky part is assessing the size of the experience gap, and the time line of the crossover and related industry shifts. There are no hard and fast ways of quantifying any of these factors. However, some proxies improve the odds of making informed judgments:

- Based on customer and competitive immersion, identify parameters for functional and experience performance. Use insights into unmet and unexpressed needs to identify missing aspects of experience performance that will give an indication of how far away from "good enough" your products (and those of your competitors) are. Usability tests will provide concrete data on the comparative experience ratings of different products.
- Use prototypes to simulate new levels of experience performance that are not possible in the current products (because of technology, price, or other constraints) to see if there are tipping points where current and potential customers suddenly start getting excited and recognizing new value. Test out different usage scenarios, capabilities that address unmet needs, and experiences that require integration of the ecosystem in different ways.
- Track the current customer base compared to total addressable market for signs that the product category is breaking into a more mainstream audience, an indicator that experience performance has reached a good enough level (this may be a trailing indicator, however, since the crossover is a precondition of mainstream adoption).
- If you have enough historical data, look for similar events in the past and how quickly the category has evolved. (Autodesk has done this with various software categories, lending more predictability to its decision making. Logitech also created a good sense for itself about timing categories.)
- Stay in continuous touch with other companies in your supply chain and ecosystem to see what trends and demands they are picking up. They may have access to a more diverse range of inputs than you.
- Look at comparative categories that have undergone similar transitions, and see if there are lessons you can learn about scope and timing of shifts.

Commoditization in a Mature Category

So far I have mostly been looking at strategic decisions around the early stage of a category, or for a company entering a category for the first time and needing to decide on the most effective innovation approaches. But what if you are in a category that seems to have matured? How do you decide if the top of the S-curve is approaching, and with it imminent decline and drastically reduced profit margins?

Evaluating one's position on the S-curve is difficult. You're in the position of a fish evaluating the water it swims in. And like many things having to do with economics, state changes can only be seen accurately in hindsight.

Here are several questions to consider as you try to evaluate the situation:

- Has the crossover point been passed so that experience quality is now exceeding what most customers need?
- Are customers becoming unwilling to pay more for either additional experience or functional performance?
- Is the game shifting from integrated to modular solutions? Are you seeing value shift from integrators to component suppliers?
- Are you in the late majority of the adoption bell curve?

If several of these are true, then the fourth scenario described earlier is playing out, where experience and functional performance are both meeting most customers' needs. This creates a low-margin commodity situation, where opportunities for differentiation are scant. To compete, you should be optimized for efficient development, incremental innovation for tactical differentiation, with strong channels for marketing and distribution. Even so, you risk disruptive threats that come from unexpected directions, as Brita's pitcher business was disrupted by bottled water. You should also be seeking out new S-curves to hop onto.

The timing of the downward spiral may still be hard to predict, but you should at least be undertaking heavy scanning of the periphery of your domain, and looking for disruptive threats and new growth opportunities.

Aligning with Organizational Temperament

Paradoxically, while customized ecosystem integration may no longer be necessary when approaching the top of the S-curve, ecosystem expansion may be one type of opportunity to pursue if it leads to the next level of complexity. If you are a company that has established itself by wrestling complex technical, business, and customer experience problems to the ground, you may not want to get caught trying to play a commodity game when integration is no longer of such value.

So build on the cost-efficiencies now available for the existing ecosystem, and expand what the ecosystem does (and the capabilities that it provides to customers) in order to reintroduce complexity and change the rules of the game. Essentially this was Progressive Insurance's method; add complexity by expanding the ecosystem (Web site, vans) of the commoditized car insurance category. Dell did it by changing the ecosystem around buying PCs, taking the commodity, modular nature of PC components as a given.

Geoffrey Moore, a long-time watcher of Silicon Valley, believes that technology companies tend to be good at either complex systems (integrators to optimize performance), or volume operations (selling large quantities of standardized products). Making the shift from one *business architecture,* as he calls it, to another is wrenching and rarely successful. Companies that thrive on complexity are better off seeking out the next level of complexity once their category has shifted to commoditized components. He cites how IBM divested itself of all its computer businesses except mainframes (which stubbornly resist modularity), and sought the next level of complexity with IT consulting services.

A classic case of not being able to shift is TiVo, which invented the digital video recorder in its Silicon Valley offices but has been unable to capitalize on the massive growth in the market.

TiVo hit the ball out of the park on both functional and experience performance with its first product, zipping straight to the crossover. This is rare, especially considering that it was converging hardware, software, and services into a single ecosystem. It achieved this so well that early customers became loyal fans.

But with the recipe established, it proved relatively simple for others to copy. The hardware components were all off-the-shelf, and knock-off user interfaces appeared from multiple companies. Cable and satellite providers were able to source DVRs from companies like Motorola and offer them almost for free, and they provided capabilities and experience performance that were "good enough." By comparison, TiVo's superior device had to be bought separately and have an additional subscription fee on top of a cable or satellite bill.

TiVo topped out at some two million subscribers and has fallen into a margin-squeezed spiral as the cable and satellite boxes expanded and then dominated the market with almost 30 million units.[21] TiVo's product was pioneering and shows the benefits of a highly convergent experience at establishing a position in the market. TiVo stayed set in an integrated mind-set, but was unable to find a way to meaningfully increase the level of complexity to hold off commodity competitors. Alternatively, if it had been able to shift to a modular mind-set and, for example, license its user interface to Motorola, it might have avoided its current situation.

So as part of your organizational immersion you want to have a clear-eyed view as to whether your company is an integrator or a component provider, and be cognizant of its true abilities to shift from one to the other if necessary.

Organization

Because of their dark-matter aspect, X-problems can lurk in an organization without being seen directly, while causing many indirect side effects. Indeed, X-problems are sometimes first recognized only by their symptoms, such as confusion over where the business is going (or even what business you are in), or over who to consider competitors, or multiple perspectives on product and market planning with no agreed-upon criteria for decisions, and numerous innovation pet projects lacking a unifying logic. Tracing these symptoms back to their root will uncover the X-problem.

Gaining insight into the X-problem requires the collaborative efforts of many people coming from different disciplines with different backgrounds and expertise. Even with the best of intentions, such diverse groups can find it hard to work together smoothly. Differing assumptions and processes, tools, and mind-sets can quickly derail effective collaboration. Throw in the fact that X-problems are ambiguous, resistant to definition, high-risk, and under time-to-market pressure, and you have a recipe for team discord and dysfunction. Jeff Conklin, who has written about similar issues with wicked problems, refers to this blame-inducing stew as *fragmentation,* because teams are pulled apart by the ambiguity of the problem definition, the social dynamics, and the technical complexity.[1]

The systemic nature of X-problems, in particular of converging ecosystems and touchpoints, causes further organizational challenges. Touchpoints and ecosystem components tend to cross over business unit boundaries. (That happens simply because customer experiences run across BU boundaries, though ideally in a way that is not evident to the customers!) The tighter integration needed for the more comprehensive experiences customers are demanding means that BUs and departments must work together in ways they never have before. The need for a rapid systeming approach means that iterative development must be coordinated across multiple groups, in contrast to rapid prototyping, which happens largely in isolation.

The famed industrial designer Raymond Loewy once said, "Design is too important to be left to designers." I would add, "Strategy is too important to be left to strategists." In other words, there are many people outside the formal role or description of strategist who should have a say in strategy. This may be an actual definitional role, or it may be simply as antennae that can inform immersion (how the world is) or adaption (what the world is becoming). It should be everyone's role to facilitate the feedback loops that are vital to adaption in a complex world. Remove the separation between planners and doers, for with X-problems the complexity is too high for any one person (or discipline) to understand or bring the necessary knowledge to the table.

o   o   o

I began by looking at what it's like to live in an X-problem world. Now it's time to see what an organization geared for solving X-problems with the Innovation X framework looks like. The subject of organizational fitness for innovation can be endless, but it is worth touching on some of the implications of Innovation X and how to accomplish immersion, convergence, divergence, and adaption.

Organizing for Immersion

In the 1960s at the height of the cold war, Soviet mathematician Pyotr Ufimtsev, chief scientist at the Moscow Institute of Radio Engineering, wrote a paper with the tantalizing title "Method of Edge Waves in the Physical Theory of Diffraction." In it, he described how to mathematically model the radar signature of an aircraft—the size and shape that the aircraft appears to be on an enemy radar. From this model, one could figure out how to minimize the signature so as to make the plane "stealthy," or almost invisible to radar. Unfortunately for the Soviets, their engineers did not recognize the paper's importance, so they were not able to capitalize on the military benefits. Ufimtsev later commented, "Senior Soviet designers were absolutely uninterested in my theories."

Nine years after the article's publication, the Air Force Foreign Technology Division finally translated it from Russian. Denys Overholser, a radar specialist in Lockheed's Skunk Works (famed creators of the U2 and SR-71 Blackbird spy planes, came across it and immediately recognized its value. Lockheed had been experimenting with stealth approaches for a while, and in fact the Blackbird incorporated some early thinking, but was far from the ideal.

Ufimtsev's paper led directly to the development of the first true stealth aircraft, the Lockheed F-117 Nighthawk, by providing the means to calculate radar effects accurately ahead of time. Until then, much of the stealth design was done by trial and error—and based on faulty assumptions, such as that the plane should have no sharp corners. In fact, the Nighthawk is famously faceted and angular, which makes it very unstable to fly. But the stealth mathematics were so effective that the radar signature of the aircraft shrank from its real sixty-five-foot length to the size of a pigeon.[2]

While most of us are not trying to figure out ways to evade enemy radar, this story illustrates that you never know where inspiration for innovation is going to come from, and that you need everyone in the organization attuned to spotting it.

Insight Is Everyone's Responsibility

Understanding the changing business context, trends, and customer needs is too important to be left to a small group of people, who will by necessity have only a constricted view. The more Jason Bournes you have out there gulping down the world, and the less you have to rely on sucking it through a straw like his government pursuers, the better.

Grant McCracken, anthropologist and marketing consultant, argues that companies should encourage all their employees to bring their own personal immersions in the outside world into the office, rather than checking them at the door, as they are often encouraged to do. "We must ask every member of the corporation to listen more carefully to the world they occupy in their off-hours, when they are removed from the citadel and out in the world. . . . A lot of cultural intelligence is already there for the asking. The trick is to improve the coverage, intensify the engagement, and capture the results."[3]

Some might say this is crowdsourcing—using the "wisdom of the crowd" to discern the future. Unfortunately X-problems are not particularly amenable to that approach, since crowdsourcing is best done with questions that have definitive answers—and, by definition, X-problems do not. But you want to prevent yourself from getting detached from the nitty-gritty of your customers' lives by overreliance on aggregated market research reports. Harnessing the observational powers of your staff helps give the inputs—if not the crowdsourced answers—to supplement the hard data.

It has a side benefit too: it gets everyone in your company customer-focused, and stepping back from their habitual processes and mind-sets enough to reflect and ask, "what should we make?"

Clif Bar — Customer Insight Every Weekend

Clif Bar uses a variety of formal and informal approaches to scan constantly for insights and opportunities. Its people at all levels benefit from being much like many of their customers: sports and outdoors enthusiasts.

CEO Gary Erickson, a trim man with close-cropped hair and a Polar heart-rate monitor watch permanently on his wrist, is an avid mountain biker. He participates in, among other races, the grueling twenty-four-hour Sea Otter Classic held annually in Monterey, California. Many of Clif's employees are also athletes. "We are the customer — we're not making widgets that nobody around here uses," he notes. "We also spend a lot of time with our customers. We go to events, go on rides, we hang out with them on a daily basis."

Clif sponsors many sporting events each year, dozens on any given weekend, and in fact 75 percent of its marketing budget goes toward grassroots initiatives rather than traditional marketing campaigns. At the events, Clif's employees act like antennae, gathering feedback from even casual observations or conversations so that the company's R&D staff can stay abreast of emerging needs and trends.[4]

But despite this constant feedback loop, the company does not blindly take inputs from customers; they are always filtered and synthesized before a new product initiative is spun up. "We do some traditional focus groups, qualitative and quantitative studies, we listen to what the trends are out there," says Erickson. "But you've got to be careful about that. What's mostly paid off for us is listening to others, but then doing our own thing."

Hire Input-Seekers

Customer input is a vital piece of any good feedback loop for effective adaption. Yet in too many companies, the conduit between customer e-mails, conversations, and other communications back to development teams is convoluted or broken.

Even if they do have structured processes, many companies look at this as a push mechanism—feeding inputs out to development teams. Amazon's Maryam Mohit says this is the wrong way to look at it. "You don't need an organization structured so the e-mails get to product developers, but rather product developers who care enough to go and get those e-mails. At Amazon.com we started out with people who cared enough to go get the information they needed. Now that we're bigger, we need those structures and processes. . . . But organization is no substitute for passion. If the people aren't passionate about the right things, your organization doesn't matter."[5]

Curiosity about customer feedback should be a hiring criterion for everyone—not just the development staff—especially if you intend to harness their observational capabilities. Curiosity should start at the top, preferably with the CEO.

Remarking on the unusual fact that Amazon's founder and CEO, Jeff Bezos, spent a week in one of the company's warehouses living the life of a stock-picker and box-packer, Saul Hansell notes that curiosity is an underrated value of a leader. He says, "I assume Mr. Bezos is curious about something, since probably a lot of things are worth a week of his time. But in my contact with Jeff Bezos over the years, I think that his restlessly inquisitive mind has been one of his most prominent and distinctive features. It's part of the origin myth of the company, in which he studied many possible online business opportunities before settling on book vendor. And it keeps showing up in the company's restless experimentation with new business ideas."[6]

McCracken recognizes that asking everyone in the organization to be antennae for new trends and innovation inspirations could result in massive information overload. But it isn't necessary to treat this all so formally. "We are not asking that everyone spend every waking moment in a scholarly study of the changes taking place in contemporary culture," he says, but just to soak things up. "Be alert to changes, patterns, possibilities, new dynamics. There won't be a quiz. No one will have to write a book report or a movie review. Just notice."[7]

It doesn't hurt to give some guidance and advice on what to look for, and how, and then make it clear what the feedback mechanisms are within the company.

For example:

- As described in Chapter Three, establish the practice of immersion tours—organized tours of cultural hot spots. Set some of these up for your staff, and use them as a way of attuning them to things to watch for.
- Give examples of customer inputs—e-mail, forum and blog posts, and the like—so that staff can see what customers are saying already. Do some what-if interpretation and extrapolation from those to think what they might imply for new innovation concepts.
- Provide staff a list of Web sites, blogs, forums, and magazines that you'd like tracked. When they have a few minutes spare they can peruse them and see what they pick up.

- Have people do presentations about themselves to their teams or groups—where they've lived, hobbies and interests, musical tastes, countries they've visited, favorite foods, prized possessions, something remarkable about themselves, previous companies and domains worked in.

We do "frogMe" presentations regularly at frog as part of Monday all-hands meetings (in contrast to "frogU" presentations, which are teaching oriented). They are a great way to discover hidden talents and interests about people you work alongside.

Organizational Implications of Convergence

Convergent ecosystems and experience touchpoints run rampant across organizational silos: R&D, marketing, sales, finance, vendors, strategic partners . . . the list goes on. It's not easy to bring these together so that they focus on the areas that are most effective. But there are things that can be done to help the process along: having the right people in place, establishing the right incentives and mind-sets, and supporting the intensive collaborative efforts required to solve X-problems.

Make the Silos Permeable

The common belief is that silos prevent innovation within companies by blocking the cross-pollination of ideas. Forrester's Bruce Temkin has the somewhat different view that silos, in and of themselves, are not the problem (and may be necessary for knowledge specialization); it's the incentives and measurements that are built up within the silos that really interfere with innovation. These tend to heighten and thicken the walls of the silos, and they focus attention and loyalty within rather than on the organization as a whole. "Incentives have to be set up right so that silos do not become overly specialized, too locally optimized. Otherwise companies get too narrow of a view of their business."[8]

Whatever their causes, silos that trap knowledge, cut off peripheral vision, and prevent collaboration are enemies to solving X-problems. Proper multi-vector immersion will likely involve multiple silos, as will tracking the periphery of the business. Insights into an X-problem may already have been uncovered within one silo but remain unknown to another, where people need it in a new context. A discarded concept that seemed stupid in one silo may cross the fine line to become very clever in another. (Texas Instruments used to give an annual prize for employees who bravely championed ideas from outside. It was called the NIHBIDIA award, or Not Invented Here But I Did It Anyway!)[9]

Autodesk has divisions that focus on broad industries (architecture, engineering and construction, media and entertainment, and design and manufacturing), but management makes sure there is also a continual cross-flow of information between the divisions. In many cases integration must occur between products within and across the industry areas. This matrixed arrangement means innovation concepts do not get stuck in one silo and can be picked up by others working in different realms of Autodesk's total domain. CTO Jeff Kowalski says this allows Autodesk to focus on a specific industry's needs but also be nimble and aware of how new concepts can be applied from one area to another. "What can we take from video game design," he asks, "and apply to bridge building?"

Multidisciplinary Teams

Earlier, in describing multi-vector research, I argued for creating interdisciplinary teams that stay together for the duration of the project. Not only does this improve the effectiveness of multi-vector research, it also streamlines the convergence of complex systems that span multiple groups and disciplines in an organization.

John Seely Brown and John Hagel observe, "When people with diverse backgrounds, experiences, and skill sets engage with each other on real problems, the exchange usually generates friction—that is, misunderstandings and arguments—before resolution and learning occur. Often this friction becomes dysfunctional; misunderstanding devolves into mistrust and opposing sides fixate on the distance between them rather than their common challenges. Yet, properly harnessed, friction can become very productive, accelerating learning, generating innovation, and fostering trust across diverse participants."[10]

Friction may be seen as a sign of inefficiency or waste, but some friction is inevitable when tackling complex problems with large amounts of ambiguity, and is a necessary step in coming to logical but unexpected insights. Handling it productively is the trick.

A hallmark of successful teams is free-flowing, nonjudgmental communication. Ed Catmull, a leader at animation studio Pixar, lays down two rules. First, everyone must be able to talk with everyone, which means not just within the team but also outside the team. People should not have to worry too much about what the "right" channels are. Second, it must be safe for everyone to offer ideas. Do people wait to reply to tricky questions until the boss has spoken? Are people belittled (explicitly or implicitly) for naive questions?[11]

I experienced this second rule at my first job out of college, as an industrial designer at Sun Microsystems. Even as the most junior employee, my opinion was honestly asked for, not just in design group meetings but also in product team meetings. There was literally no sense that hierarchy of titles and years at the company should dictate who could or could not contribute to a product design problem. The attitude at Sun was, "The more brains, the better."

In hindsight, for someone so inexperienced I was given an astonishing amount of autonomy and responsibility by the design group's manager, Phil Yurkonis, and my mentor, Mike Antonczak. As a manager today, I must dampen the feelings of uneasiness that can sometimes creep in when delegating to junior staff on important projects. But if you've been smart with hiring, and you have safety nets in place, then delegation should have minimal risk, and it will give junior staff opportunities to learn. And who knows, you may get a breakthrough idea because someone did what they didn't know they weren't supposed to be able to do.

At frog we frequently staff projects with teams of people from multiple disciplines and industry experience backgrounds, even when the project focus nominally falls into a specific realm, such as software or hardware, consumer electronics or transportation. While this may seem wasteful and inefficient, we have found it to be *the* most effective way of coming up with unexpected insights and innovations. Rather than seeing the provision of multiple and seemingly redundant perspectives as an expense, we see it as an investment—the most reliable way to understand complex problems quickly and to come up with the most provocative and relevant solutions.

For the same reason, we do not have verticals for industry specialization. We would risk establishing silos that block the sharing of perspectives and experience. Instead we have expert groups that meet and converse regularly, and that share information on the internal wiki. But these live outside the organizational structure and cut across disciplines and offices.

Get the Whole System in One Room

I remember attending a meeting at a manufacturer of videoconferencing hardware for which teams were joining from several remote locations. It was a point of pride with the company that it could showcase its products this way. Unfortunately, getting everything working took a precious thirty minutes—and this was at the company's headquarters, using its products, calling its own staff at its own facilities! Digital communications can help close distances, but anyone who has survived lengthy e-mail threads, phone tag, disruptive instant message conversations, and 6 A.M. teleconferences knows that they are no substitute for getting the whole team together physically in their immersive space.

There is great value in processing large quantities of information in a single collaborative space, using physical artifacts like Post-it notes and whiteboards. Unfortunately this is a luxury at most companies, where buildings are designed for either long-term solo work (offices and cubicles) or short periods of group meetings (conference rooms). Most office buildings are just not set up to properly support the kind of collaborative work that X-problems require. Companies need to adjust their priorities of space planning to dedicate more space to rooms for prolonged group collaboration.

Distance matters. People are wired to interact directly with other people, unmediated by technology, and are much more effective when they can do this firsthand, spontaneously, as needed. Even the barrier of a floor or a separation of as little as ten meters can make a dramatic difference to the frequency of communication among team members. Preston Smith argues that team members need to be within earshot of one another to be fully effective, and a University of Michigan study found that co-located teams were twice as productive as dispersed teams. Problems got solved quicker, learning was more effective, perspectives could be shared and contested more easily, and junior members could absorb the lessons of their seniors.[12]

At frog we will sometimes have clients, especially Asian companies, who want to co-locate with our teams in a frog studio, often for weeks at a time. Their intent is to learn the innovation process, not just be handed new concepts. Why go to that trouble? Because they recognize that there is no better way to understand the subtleties of crunching X-problems than by taking part in the process firsthand.

I realize that true co-location is difficult, if not impossible, for many companies to accomplish all the time. (At frog we too will run projects across studios when necessary.) At minimum, people should work together within their locations in multidisciplinary groups, and should all meet in person at the beginning of a project so that they have time to bond. This should include social activities so that guards come down, and people learn about each other as *people* rather than as colleagues. Building trust is critical, as at times discussions will get heated, preconceptions challenged, and discomfort levels will rise. Personal trust is what prevents those spilling over into acrimony and dysfunctional friction, as Brown and Hagel warn about.

Organizational Implications of Divergence

I talked at the beginning of the book about how X-problems are a specific variant of wicked problems. A common approach to wicked problems, especially given their prevalence in social planning and policy settings, is to focus on facilitation techniques to bring about shared understanding of the problem. While in the case of X-problems we aim to outwit competitors in our understanding, with wicked problems the goal is to have a mutually beneficial alignment and support of the problem definition. But within an X-problem team, it is often necessary to manage alignment and shared perspectives just as it is for stakeholders in wicked problems. Team members should not be competing against each other for insights and solutions (unless the team is consciously and purposefully set up this way in order to stir creative friction); they should be working for their mutual benefit.

In finding the balance in divergence of the core business and venturing into new areas, considerable social strains will be put on the organization. If left unmanaged, the ambiguity and complexity of the X-problem will cause disagreements and unfocused, uncoordinated, and redundant efforts. As different groups and disciplines go to work on the problem, they can fragment along organizational lines, or into factions based on their shared understanding and perceptions of the problem.

Conklin uses the term *coherence* as the counterpoint to this fragmentation. A coherent team has a shared understanding about the various perceptions, beliefs, information, and approaches to the problem. This does not mean the members necessarily reach consensus, but that each person (or discipline, group, or organization) recognizes how others may be seeing and approaching the X-problem differently. Conklin emphasizes the importance of conscious, structured sessions to tease out the variety of perspectives and develop a clearly articulated definition of purpose and the challenges ahead. With this foundation acting as an externalized touchstone, when friction does occur, it can be harnessed rather than turning into frustrating wheel-spinning.

Several key pieces of knowledge need to be widely understood throughout the organization to provide the best foundation for responding to X-problems:

- *Domain scope:* Do people at all levels throughout your organization really understand what your domain is? Without it, they are shooting blind when it comes to initiating innovation efforts. Managers may assume that everyone knows the intellectual property held by the company, what its core competencies and insights are, who it partners with, what areas of the ecosystem it plays in, what needs it satisfies for customers, and who its customers are. Too often this is not actually the case, and staff have only a vague and perhaps even misguided understanding.

- *Organizational strengths:* The discussion of Logitech illustrated some of its clear organizational strengths. These strengths do not dictate strategy, nor exactly which markets to go into, but they provide a conceptual decision-making framework. On the other hand, other companies discussed here have let their strengths fall into a state of benign neglect. This makes the situation seem hopeless, as there is no apparent foundation to build on. In this case, it is necessary to rediscover and reenergize a company's strengths.

Establish the Panic Threshold

Earlier, I mentioned Wayne Gretsky and his high panic threshold, his patience at waiting for just the right opening to come along. It is important with X-problems that the panic threshold be set high enough to avoid prematurely taming the problems, calling them solved when in fact they are not. Individual teams tackling X-problems will have to calibrate their own panic thresholds, but it is also important that the organization have an overall feel for how far it is willing to go with entertaining radical, disruptive ideas.

Companies at the top of an industry S-curve—the ones emerging out of the mature middle and now facing volatility as their category disintegrates—are apt to be stuck in a mind-set of incremental change: small innovations to existing products selling to familiar customers against known competitors. All these boundaries are swept away when flying off the top of the curve. In this newly dynamic environment, the companies find themselves unfit for radical innovation.

Leadership must step up and set the expectations about the new panic threshold, and then must live up to it with courageous decisions.

Some of these will work out, others won't; but that also sets the expectation that mistakes, if learned from, are now also tolerated, even encouraged (if they are treated as food for the next round of work).

But if organizational metrics do not shift along with the rhetoric, then the words will ultimately have little lasting effect. Process stage-gates, evaluation metrics, market projections, and so on all need to be reevaluated for radical innovations, or ideas will get killed prematurely because they exceed the old panic threshold intended for incremental innovation. (As a corollary, there should be a "minimum panic threshold" too. Sort of like the roller-coaster signs that say "You must be this tall to ride," when aiming for radical innovation you need an expectation of exceeding business as usual.)

Gary Erickson recalls a time when Clif Bar's normal market checks were not providing conclusive enough guidance for a new, highly innovative product that had enjoyed an exceptionally long gestation period. He exclaimed, "This product is coming out by the end of the year. I don't care what focus groups say or what consumer research says, I'm betting on this thing. It just needs to happen."

This type of executive mandate is required surprisingly often to push ideas through new product development process stage-gates tuned for small improvements to existing products, which tend to block more radical innovations. One study by Deloitte and *The Economist* revealed that though many executives see the need for different metrics for evaluating radical innovation efforts, only a few companies have established parallel stage-gate paths for them. Furthermore, almost half of executives have at some point needed to use "clandestine" or "underground" methods to push through innovation efforts that were getting stalled by the usual formal processes.[13] The damn-the-torpedoes conviction that Erickson showed can be necessary to grow an innovation portfolio in the riskier, more forward-thinking direction, and keep it from getting stuck in short-term incrementalism.

The opposite danger to incrementalism also exists: setting growth targets that are unreasonably high for the nascent and possibly niche new markets. Think of this as *gigantism:* companies used to fat profit margins and large customer bases may have a distorted idea of what they can realistically achieve with seed innovation efforts. At frog we had one client who was looking to branch out of its saturated market to find new growth areas. It had dubbed the approach "big baby" because it could start small but had to grow up and get big very quickly, on the order of hundreds of millions of dollars in just a few years. Those kinds of opportunities are not just sitting out in plain sight.

The same Deloitte study showed that almost half of executives surveyed required at least an 11 percent to 20 percent increase in revenues from an innovation effort within three years of market launch, and significant numbers of them wanted *more than* a 20 percent increase. Furthermore, almost half of the executives wanted positive cash flow on the innovations within two years of launch. Those are some tough parameters, and they tend to force an emphasis on what seem to be "safer" bets in established markets rather than "risky" bets in new markets, with the assumption that those will yield more predictable returns.[14]

Product developers subscribe to the old saying: There are three variables—good, fast, and cheap—but you only get to pick two at a time. Opportunity finding is the same way. If it's a good, immediately available opportunity, it is not going to be cheap to capitalize on. It will require investment to build it up, get the word out to large numbers of customers, and perhaps displace incumbents who are serving the same or similar needs. Good opportunities can be pursued at lower cost, but will require more patience to reach full scale.

Avoid Innovation Culture Split

A common approach to fostering radical innovation, experimenting with new business areas, and bypassing conventional metrics is to set up a distinct innovation hothouse or Skunk Works – type group whose sole purpose is to "think outside the box," revenues be damned (for now).

Rosabeth Moss Kanter cautions that this can quickly lead to a split of cultures: one group is having all the fun, and the other is making all the money. "The designated innovators, whether an R&D group or a new-venture unit, are identified as creators of the future. They are free of rules or revenue demands and are allowed to play with ideas that don't yet work. Their colleagues are expected to follow rules, meet demands, and make money while feeling like grinds and sometimes being told they are dinosaurs whose business models will soon be obsolete."[15] This is a recipe for organizational dysfunction.

Separate, centralized innovation groups have their place, but the recent trend of open innovation should encourage you to consider alternative models.

Divergence Is Everyone's Business

In their study of Google's "innovation machine," Iyer and Davenport note how innovation is built into job descriptions at the company, and is budgeted for explicitly in employee time with the every-Friday rule (amounting to 20 percent of people's time—though in reality it is not literally every Friday as the time can be taken in chunks). The innovations they work on are known as "20 percent projects." Managers also must spend time on innovation, dedicating 70 percent to core business, 20 percent to expansion efforts, and 10 percent to entirely new business and products.[16]

With 20 percent projects, Google tackles two thorny problems that have plagued other approaches to fostering divergent innovations at the periphery of the business.

First, it addresses the problem of converting from the "rubber meets the sky" of corporate R&D labs to the "rubber meets the road" of product development, which has been a hit-or-miss proposition at best. The centralized labs of Xerox, IBM, NEC and others have uneven records of technology transfer and enabling marketable breakthrough innovations. The old-guard companies with legacy labs have been upstaged by newer companies: Cisco beat Lucent, Nokia beat Motorola, Intel beat IBM. As Henry Chesbrough puts it, we are shifting from a world where innovation requires control (that is, centralization and proprietary ownership) to one where innovation requires openness (decentralization and mutual benefits).[17]

Second, it encourages all engineers to act as antennae for new innovations that address unmet customer needs at the edges of the business. It greatly expands Google's peripheral vision. It is a radically bottom-up approach, but one paired with a top-down funnel that aligns innovations to the business objectives (the Top 100 list mentioned in Chapter Seven). This ensures relevance, and improves effectiveness. According to Marissa Mayer, VP of research, more than fifty new products have emerged out of these personal projects, including Gmail, AdSense, and Google News.

Helping come up with innovative products should be part of everyone's job at a company, argues Gary Erickson. He says that at Clif Bar, "We bonus people based on how well we've reached our innovation goals, how well we've reached our environmental and community service goals. We have these metrics on everybody's goals. We don't just give bonuses based on profit."

Organizational Implications of Adaption

Adaption is difficult for organizations to deal with because it involves prolonged ambiguity. How do you know if you are heading down a successful path, and what success will look like at the end? With X-problems, neither of these questions has a clear-cut answer. This is why companies often oscillate between sticking too long with a vision and adjusting it too frequently based on customer feedback. Recognizing the promise of a new idea ahead of time can be very difficult, but once it is proven, then competitors will jump in with their own versions.

Movies and television are two industries that constantly seek out novel ideas (as long as they can be assured of success) along with milking proven ideas for as long as possible.

Here is a quick quiz: Which TV show proposal was initially rejected by the networks, before it became a hit?

- *Desperate Housewives*
- *Survivor*
- *American Idol*
- *CSI*

Answer: All of the above. None of these four shows was initially recognized (except wishfully by their creators) as a potential hit. CBS president Leslie Moonves thought *Survivor* was the dumbest show he'd ever heard of. At first. A lower-level executive kept pressing him, and he gradually came around. Rupert Murdoch had to intervene (at his daughter's behest) to bring *American Idol* to air on Fox, despite an equivalent show's success in the U.K. ABC developed *CSI* but then chose not to run it, which became their loss and CBS's gain. *Desperate Housewives* required endless attempts to find a studio that got the concept. Someone of influence had to see the promise of each of these shows and shepherd it to the airwaves.[18]

Once each show became a success, it was followed by a string of copycat shows. These competitors had the benefit of empirical evidence, while the pioneers who launched the four shows only had intuition.

Or did they? We often use the word "intuition" disparagingly, treating it as barely different from a wild guess. How intuition works is quite mysterious, but the fact is that some people can connect their past experiences and gain insight into novel situations. Companies pay big dollars to people with good intuition who have the pulse of mass culture and niche audiences alike. People like Geoffrey Frost, who intuited changing perceptions of cell phones ahead of the rest of the industry. I call this *pattern experience*.

Pattern Experience

X-problems are understood only vaguely early on, so having an ability to see patterns is a shortcut to a more precise problem definition.[19] Karl Weick describes this as a retroactive process of sense-making; that is, making sense of situations after they have occurred, in order to better handle them as they occur in the future. Reflection and sense-making of previous successes, failures, and experiments are vital for an organization looking to improve its feedback loops.[20]

Chess grand masters are people who have accumulated pattern experience. They have honed their abilities to sense where patterns of pieces on a board are going to lead. This is how they can play dozens of other players of lesser skill level simultaneously; they don't need to memorize every piece, only the broad pattern for each game. Deep knowledge of gambits is modified as needed for each emergent situation, making quick work of cutting complex problems down to size.

Most chess moves on a professional level are decided upon in less than a minute; the rest of the time is spent confirming the soundness of the decision. This happens when doing analysis on X-problems too: you want people on the job who can get that early intuitive feel for the problem and where it is leading, even if they cannot articulate it right away. Much of their time is spent analyzing the intuited hypotheses in detail.

Being able to spot patterns early and understand their implications is part intuition and part years of experience. It is important that people with lots of pattern experience are dispersed throughout an organization and work closely with staff who have less experience. This way the patterns get passed on through collaboration. Combine the old hands with "naive" staff who are not afraid of asking dumb questions and challenging the received wisdom.

A common way for pattern experiences to get passed on is through stories: people recounting successes and failures, humorous events, or painful lessons they've learned.

In their book *Made to Stick,* Chip and Dan Heath say stories are how we get people to act on our ideas. They give the example of firefighters swapping stories, each tale serving to multiply the experience of the listeners. Stories are *sticky,* as they put it, in a way that dry accounts of facts, or statistics, or research reports are not. We put ourselves in the place of the storyteller and amplify our knowledge in the process. The Heaths say, "Research shows that mentally rehearsing a situation helps us perform better when we encounter that situation in the physical environment. Similarly, hearing stories acts as a kind of mental flight simulator, preparing us to respond more quickly and effectively."[21]

Sometimes the stories bear only a passing connection to the business at hand, but become powerful analogies for how the organization should conduct itself. Clif Bar's Erickson uses stories a lot to communicate the values of the company and to keep its origin story alive. He tells one story about a time he was ice climbing in Yosemite, and lost both his ice ax (necessary for upward movement as well as catching downward slides) and the metal spikes fitted to his boots. But he was in such a position that he had to keep going to the summit, despite the risk of falling. He uses the story to illustrate three qualities: being *attentive* to the surrounding context and *adapting* to emerging situations, and the need to take *action* in the face of uncertainty.

He says, "For me, stories are useful for a couple of reasons. First is, I'm not very technical when it comes to business. I can talk a bit of techno-language and theory, but it's boring. Second, people relate to and remember stories. Their eyes roll back in their heads when you start talking theory. People are engaged and inspired by stories and parables."[22]

Reduce Risk with Experimentation

When I was in high school I did hurdles on the track team. Our coach, Mr. Cruz, liked to talk about the hurdling event as a metaphor for life: developing a smooth, uninterrupted flow so one's pace stays constant despite any barriers put in one's way.

Unfortunately, we only had ancient wooden hurdles that were so heavy they didn't budge at all when you whacked them with your trailing knee. It only took one painful impact of your kneecap against the unyielding hurdle to deter further experimentation. When Mr. Cruz exhorted us to lengthen our strides and go lower over the hurdles, we all ignored him and played it safe. This put us at a significant disadvantage when we competed against runners who had practiced on modern featherweight hurdles. We just didn't have the technique to keep up, hobbled (literally and figuratively) as we were by our outdated equipment.

But it was the pole vaulters who were the crazy ones. The thing about pole vaulting is that you have to try it in order to do it—you can't read a book and then walk up and make a successful vault. You have to give it a run, and then fall. And you have to keep failing, again and again, until eventually you figure out how to do it. But there are things you can do to mitigate the consequences of failure. You can start with very small jumps, or hold the pole just part of the way up and not do its full bend. You can put big cushions around to soften the inevitable fall.

The issue for an organization is not so much avoiding risk—risk will find you whether you seek it out or not. The key is making it safe for your staff to take risks. Your organization needs the resiliency to recover from temporary setbacks and the ability to turn failures into food for new efforts, so that you gradually improve as you shed light on the dark matter of the X-problem.

Truths

This book started with the question, Why isn't innovation working? Organizations are being tested in extreme ways in a world of disruptive competition, ever more demanding customers, the need to deliver integrated systems of offerings, and the challenge of ambiguous, emergent goals. The Innovation X framework provides a comprehensive set of methods for analyzing and acting on these challenges.

By way of conclusion, here are four basic truths about what it takes to succeed with X-problems and to carry out the Innovation X methods effectively. Some are truisms, yet they bear repeating. (If they are so widely known, why are they still so widely *not* done well?) Others are perhaps elephants in the room that no one wants to acknowledge.

Truth 1: Customer experience is everyone's business

It is common wisdom in service companies that customer service is everyone's responsibility. Nonetheless, the people on the front line—the ones actually serving and talking with customers—are at the end of a long chain of decisions, mechanisms, and structures that put constraints on how well they can provide service. Choices made months, even years, before can have a profound effect on the perceived quality of service.

Customer experience as it applies to convergent systems of hardware, software, and services (or any of these individually for that matter) is similar. The nuances of end-user experiences reflect larger decisions about strategy, business model, outsourcing, development process, empathy for customers' needs, brand, and organizational values. Not only is there a link in terms of development, but customers will pick up on it too, rewarding you when they like their experience, and shunning and disparaging you when they don't. These days, much of that appreciation and disparagement will happen publicly, on a global scale, thanks to the Web.

Forrester's Bruce Temkin argues that customer experience should be everyone's responsibility, not just that of a specific group or division. He says, "Customer experience today is like the quality movement back in the 80s. There was a time when quality was created as a department, with a Chief Quality Officer. But people found that this meant that the rest of the organization spent *less* time worrying about quality, as they assumed someone else was taking care of it. The same challenge applies to customer experience. It needs to be pervasive throughout the organization so that the whole organization becomes customer-centric."

Customer experience is too vital in an X-problem world to leave to a small group of specialists. The customer experience mentality must be top-of-mind for everyone, even if they are not the expert crafters and developers of the actual touchpoints.

Truth 2: Not everything that counts can be counted, and not everything that can be counted, counts

This basic truth comes from a sign in Einstein's office at Princeton. I find it a nice counterpoint to the oft-stated belief that you cannot manage what you cannot measure. As tidy as life would be if measure-and-manage were in fact true, unfortunately there are important factors that stubbornly resist—for now—easy measurement.

A free-spirited innovation culture has thrived at 3M, particularly in the R&D labs, in spite of the company's rather stodgy, non-flashy public persona. When a new outsider CEO arrived in 2000 and started to apply Six Sigma efficiency processes, his buttoned-down, analysis-driven methods clashed with 3M's culture of flexibility.

A *Business Week* article about the shift observed, "The very factors that make Six Sigma effective in one context can make it ineffective in another. Traditionally, it uses rigorous statistical analysis to produce unambiguous data that help produce better quality, lower costs, and more efficiency. That all sounds great when you know what outcomes you'd like to control. But what about when there are few facts to go on—or you don't even know the nature of the problem you're trying to define?" In other words, when you're dealing with X-problems. Research suggests that quality programs tend to bias innovation to the incremental rather than radical, causing a worrying imbalance in the innovation portfolio.

Art Fry, the inventor of Post-it notes, observes that innovation is a numbers game. He adds, "You have to go through 5,000 to 6,000 raw ideas to find one successful business." This is something that organizations primarily focused on efficiency have a hard time accommodating. In fact, early in the Six Sigma effort at 3M, technical employees concluded that the Post-it note would never have emerged from such a process.

With the arrival of George Buckley as CEO in 2005, the strictures around Six Sigma appear to have loosened. "Invention is by its very nature a disorderly process," he says. "You can't put a Six Sigma process into that area and say, 'well, I'm getting behind on invention, so I'm going to schedule myself for three good ideas on Wednesday and two on Friday.' That's not how creativity works."[1]

Truth 3: Talent matters

The unavoidable truth is that when solving difficult problems, you need to have bright and creative people on the case. You need a combination of visionaries and ditch-diggers, stubborn idealists and open-minded pragmatists, people who seek ambiguity and broadening options, and people who strive for clarity and option reduction. It's the magical interplay of these characteristics, often sifted on a person-by-person basis, that makes up an effective team. (In other words, people are not interchangeable by role—their specific backgrounds and personalities do matter.)

Ed Catmull at Pixar argues, "If you want to be original, you have to accept [risk], even when it's uncomfortable, and have the capability to recover when your organization takes a big risk and fails. What's the key to being able to recover? Talented people!" Unfortunately, talented people are hard to find. But the benefits are worth waiting for. "If you give a good idea to a mediocre team, they will screw it up; if you give a mediocre idea to a great team, they will either fix it or throw it away and come up with something that works."[2]

At frog design we hire less than 1 percent of the people who apply for positions at the company. Every applicant goes through several rounds of interviews and meets with a range of people—senior and junior, in their discipline and outside it. They must demonstrate clear superiority in their expertise, be quick on their feet when thinking about problems they've never encountered before, and be comfortable working in highly multidisciplinary teams. They must be a good personality fit for their team as well as the studio and the frog culture overall. Very few people fit that profile, but it is only by being highly selective that we are able to ensure consistent top performance.

Beyond talent in a particular area, other attributes are also important:

- *Curiosity* . . . about new ideas, new fields, new people, and the willingness to seek them out and soak them up.
- *Caring about customers* . . . not just lip service, but the astuteness to observe, discuss, empathize, reason with, and truly understand customers, and then translate that into innovations that are relevant.
- *Good at playing with others* . . . who may not have similar expertise, but who are collectively vital to helping get the job done.
- *Flexibility* . . . of processes, methods, conceptual frameworks; know when to go to the mat for an idea, and when to compromise.

- *Comfort with ambiguity*... not leaping to conclusions, jumping straight from observing something to thinking of a solution; be satisfied with prolonging the period of not-knowing, while still acting and producing in the meantime.
- *Good at spotting patterns*... able to think inductively (developing reusable theories and patterns out of individual cases), deductively (recognizing when an existing framework applies to an emerging, ambiguous situation), and abductively (working off intuitive hunches to create initial hypotheses).

Truth 4: It starts at the top

Leading an organization living through an X-problem is stressful and difficult. If you are reacting to fleeing customers, stagnating market share and margins, and unexpected competitors, the pain is manifold. The ambiguity and risk are deeply worrying.

You as a leader set the tone for how these changes are handled. Will you be more like Jeff Bezos, whose endless curiosity leads him to spend a week in the warehouse? Like Clif Bar's Gary Erickson, who gets out and plays alongside his customers? Or like the phone company executives who have lost touch with their customers' needs because they do not even use the products they sell?

Will you have the courage to try new things, accept mistakes if they are learned from productively, and wait patiently to see which seeds blossom into strong new opportunities?

Will you encourage and support people to do the hard things, as John F. Kennedy put it, *because* they are hard, because by doing them you will achieve a more meaningful and true differentiation, and take your company to heights only dreamed of?

Difficulty, complexity, interdependence, ambiguity, risk—these are not things to be avoided in an X-problem world; they must be embraced. It is only by taking them on that you will outwit the competition with valuable but unexpected products that charm their way into customers' hearts.

Notes

Introduction

1 Jonathan Copulsky and Ken Hutt, "Gambling with the House's Money: The Randomness of Corporate Innovation" (Chicago: Deloitte, 2006).

2 Geoffrey A. Moore, *Dealing with Darwin: How Great Companies Innovate at Every Phase of Their Evolution* (New York: Portfolio, 2006), Chapter 4.

3 There are numerous taxonomies of innovation. For example, see Paul Trott, *Innovation Management and New Product Development* (Essex, England: Pearson Education, 2008), pp. 10 – 15; Tony Davila, Marc J. Epstein, and Robert D. Shelton, *Making Innovation Work: How to Manage It, Measure It, and Profit from It* (Upper Saddle River, NJ: Wharton School, 2006), Chapter 2. My goal here is not to arrive at a definitive definition, but more to box in the general area that the book deals with.

4 I have stayed away from the term *disruptive* at the upper end as that is often defined specifically as a business model innovation that cannibalizes existing business models. Many people do use the word to describe any kind of innovation that is transformatively different, but it seems clearer to avoid it.

Prologue

1 Carly Fiorina, *Tough Choices* (New York: Penguin, 2006), p. 183.

Chapter 1   Living in an X-Problem World

1 Clayton M. Christensen and Michael E. Raynor, *The Innovator's Solution: Creating and Sustaining Successful Growth* (Boston: Harvard Business Press, 2003), p. 73.

2 Economist Intelligence Unit, "The Innovators: How Successful Companies Drive Business Transformation," *The Economist* (2008), p. 24.

3 Carl Bass, Jeff Kowalski, and Brian Mathews, interview with author, January 7, 2009.

4 Chris Gaither, "Google Puts Lid on New Products; Realizing That Its Myriad Services Are Confusing Users, It Will Focus on Refining What It Has," *Los Angeles Times,* October 6, 2006.

5 Tony Davila, Marc J. Epstein, and Robert D. Shelton, *Making Innovation Work: How to Manage It, Measure It, and Profit from It* (Upper Saddle River, NJ: Wharton School, 2006), p. 71.

6 E. Jeffrey Conklin, *Dialogue Mapping: Building Shared Understanding of Wicked Problems* (Hoboken, NJ: Wiley, 2006).

7 For instance, see J. C. Camillus, "Strategy as a Wicked Problem," *Harvard Business Review* 86, no. 5 (2008): 98; Marty Neumeier, *The Designful Company* (Berkeley, CA: Peachpit Press, 2008).

8 Rittel and Webber had a more binary categorization: tame versus wicked problems. The simple/complex/wicked categorization comes from Nancy Roberts, an instructor at the Monterey Naval Post-Graduate School, and I find it more useful. See Nancy Roberts, "Coping with Wicked Problems: The Case of Afghanistan," *Learning from International Public Management Reform* 11B (2001): 353 – 355; David S. Luckey and Kevin P. Schultz, "Defining and Coping with Wicked Problems: The Case of Fort Ord Building Removal" (Monterey, CA: Naval Post-Graduate School, March, 2001), p. 2.

9 This definition of wicked problems is consolidated from a number of sources, each of which gives a slightly different treatment. See H.W.J. Rittel, "On the Planning Crisis: Systems Analysis of 'The First and Second

Generations,'" *Bedriftsokonomen,* No. 8 (1972): 392 – 393; Conklin, *Dialogue Mapping,* pp. 14 – 16; Luckey and Schultz, "Defining and Coping with Wicked Problems," pp. 2 – 3.

10 Gary Hamel, *Leading the Revolution* (Boston: Harvard Business Press, 2002), p. 292.

11 Grant McCracken, "Innovations for the Innovator," This Blog Sits at the Intersection of Anthropology and Economics, October 24, 2006; retrieved from www.cultureby.com/trilogy/2006/10/innovators_inno.html, August 7, 2009.

12 Stephen Jay Gould, *Full House* (New York: Three Rivers Press, 1996), 89 – 128.

13 "Global CEO Study, 2008: The Enterprise of the Future," IBM, May 2008, p. 25. Retrieved from http://ibm.com/ibm/ideasfromibm/us/ceo /20080505/, September 16, 2009.

14 Daniel H. Pink, *A Whole New Mind: Moving from the Information Age to the Conceptual Age* (New York: Riverhead Books, 2005), p. 33.

15 Bruce D. Temkin, "Customer Experience Correlates to Loyalty" (Cambridge, MA: Forrester, February 17, 2009).

16 "Global CEO Study, 2008," p. 37.

Chapter 2   The Innovation X Framework

1 Some people will look at this list and think I am describing design research. But there is very little agreement on what *design research* encompasses. Some people treat it purely as qualitative user research, whereas others, myself included, see it as having much broader potential. And calling something *design* research can make it sound like only designers are involved in doing it, when just the opposite should be true. So I am using the more neutral term *immersion.*

2 Karl Weick argues that learning is not possible without acting: the world makes sense in the process of acting on it. Henry Mintzberg, Bruce Ahlstrand, and Joseph Lampel, *Strategy Safari* (New York: Free Press, 2005), pp. 195 – 199.

3 Gary Hamel and C. K. Prahalad, "The Core Competence of the Corporation," *Harvard Business Review* 68, no. 3 (1990): 79 – 91.

4 Clayton M. Christensen and Michael E. Raynor, *The Innovator's Solution: Creating and Sustaining Successful Growth* (Boston: Harvard Business Press, 2003), p. 162.

5 "Fuck Everything, We're Doing Five Blades," *The Onion,* February 18, 2004; retrieved from www.theonion.com/content/node/33930, August 7, 2009.

6 "Gillette Unveils 5-Bladed Razor," CNN Money, September 14, 2005; retrieved from http://money.cnn.com/2005/09/14/news/fortune500 /gillette/, August 5, 2009.

Chapter 3   Immersion

1 The Bourne chase scenario shares many of the same attributes as the Millennium Challenge war game described by Malcolm Gladwell in *Blink.* In the $250 million simulation, a U.S. general named Van Riper led a fictional guerrilla force of Middle Eastern fighters against a massively equipped U.S. force. The U.S. team were "gorging on information" as Gladwell put it, but doing so from a remote location with lots of sensors, just like Bourne's pursuers. Van Riper's far smaller team was on the ground and behaving in highly unexpected ways. The Middle Eastern guerrillas were, in simulation, able to avoid detection and quickly decimate the U.S. warship fleet. The result was so embarrassing that the simulation was reset and the rules rigged to give more advantage to the U.S. forces. Malcolm Gladwell, *Blink: The Power of Thinking Without Thinking* (New York: Little, Brown, 2005).

2 Henry Mintzberg, Bruce Ahlstrand, and Joseph Lampel, *Strategy Safari* (New York: Free Press, 2005), pp. 69, 71.

3 Mintzberg, Ahlstrand, and Lampel, *Strategy Safari*, pp. 60, 71.

4 Carl Bass, Jeff Kowalski, and Brian Mathews, interview with author, January 7, 2009.

5 Others have also used the peripheral vision metaphor. There's even a whole book using the analogy: George S. Day and Paul J. H. Schoemaker, *Peripheral Vision: Detecting the Weak Signals That Will Make or Break Your Company* (Boston: Harvard Business Press, 2006). Michael E. McGrath devotes a chapter to different vision analogies in *Product Strategy for High*

Technology Companies: Accelerating Your Business to Web Speed (New York: McGraw-Hill, 2001), pp. 3 – 14.

6   Designers, in particular, often take *research* to mean only "user research." There is a notion of "design research" that focuses on qualitative research on small numbers of users (often leading-edge users who represent the extremes of product usage and behaviors), and that is purposefully contrasted with traditional secondary research techniques used by marketing, but again "design research" often is almost exclusively focused on user research.

7   Julie Anixter, Interview with the author, March 11, 2009.

8   For more on the lead user approach, see Eric von Hippel, *Democratizing Innovation* (Cambridge, MA: MIT Press, 2005); Eric von Hippel, "Lead Users: A Source of Novel Product Concepts," *Management Science* 32, no. 7 (1986): 791 – 805; Eric von Hippel, Stefan Thomke, and Mary Sonnack, "Creating Breakthroughs at 3M," *Harvard Business Review* 77, no. 5 (1999): 47; Day and Schoemaker, *Peripheral Vision,* pp. 53 – 56; and Emanuel Rosen, *The Anatomy of Buzz: How to Create Word-of-Mouth Marketing* (New York: Doubleday Business, 2002), pp. 43 – 57.

9   "Global CEO Study, 2008: The Enterprise of the Future," IBM, May 2008, p. 25. One CEO cited said, "In the future, we will be talking more and more about the 'prosumer'—a consumer/producer who is even more extensively integrated into the value chain. As a consequence, production processes will be customized more precisely and individually." Retrieved from http://ibm.com/ibm/ideasfromibm/us/ceo/20080505/, September 16, 2009.

10 Smith cites a study by Alan MacCormack (of Harvard Business School) and Barry Boehm (of the University of Southern California) about the value of early prototyping and customer feedback: Preston G. Smith, *Flexible Product Development: Building Agility for Changing Markets* (San Francisco: Jossey-Bass, 2007), pp. 34 – 36. For some excellent examples of early-stage concepting, see William Buxton, *Sketching User Experiences: Getting the Design Right and the Right Design* (San Francisco: Morgan Kaufmann, 2007).

11 Mary Walton, *Car* (New York: Norton, 1999), pp. 45 – 46.

12 Smith, *Flexible Product Development,* p. 50.

13 Bruce Temkin, Interview with the author, March 10, 2009.

14 Mihaly Csikszentmihalyi, *Flow: The Psychology of Optimal Experience* (New York: HarperPerennial, 1991).

15 "Meet MAX: IPC Launches New Desktop Designed by Traders for Traders," IPC press release, March 15, 2006; retrieved from http://ipc.com/repository/document/277.pdf, August 17, 2009.

16 From the frog design Web site www.frogdesign.com/pdf/frog_design_ipc.pdf.

17 Penguin Books, "About Penguin: Company History," Penguin UK Web site, n.d.; retrieved from www.penguin.co.uk/static/packages/uk/aboutus/history.html, August 7, 2009.

18 Mark Hurst, "Interview: Maryam Mohit, Amazon.Com," November 21, 2002; retrieved from www.goodexperience.com/blog/archives/000192.php, August 6, 2009.

19 Anthony Ulwick, *What Customers Want* (New York: McGraw-Hill, 2005), p. xxv.

Chapter 4 Convergence

1 Bruce D. Temkin, "Customer Experience Correlates to Loyalty" (Cambridge, MA: Forrester, February 17, 2009).

2 Bruce Temkin, "Brands Are Dying; Deal with It," Forrester, March 6, 2009. Retrieved from http://experiencematters.wordpress.com/2009/03/06/brands-are-dying-deal-with-it/, August 8, 2009.

3 Christopher Vollmer, "Digital Darwinism," *Strategy+Business,* no. 54 (Spring 2009): 66.

4 A fair amount has been written recently about how to use small incentives to gently encourage beneficial behaviors. For example, see Daniel J. Goldstein, Eric J. Johnson, Andreas Herrmann, and Mark Heitmann, "Nudge Your Customers Toward Better Choices," *Harvard Business Review* 86, no. 12 (2008): 99 – 105; and Richard H. Thaler and Cass R. Sunstein, *Nudge: Improving Decisions About Health, Wealth, and Happiness* (New Haven, CT: Yale University Press, 2008).

5   Myra Hart, Michael Roberts, and Julia Stevens, "Zipcar: Refining the Business Model," Harvard Business School Case no. 9-803-09, 2005: pp. 6 – 9.

6   Hart, Roberts, and Stevens, "Zipcar: Refining the Business Model," p. 6.

7   Daniel Imhoff, *Paper or Plastic* (San Francisco: Sierra Club Books, 2005), pp. 58 – 59.

Chapter 5   Divergence

1   "Water Filtration in the United States, 2008" (Dublin, Ireland: Research and Markets, 2008).

2   Gary Hamel, *Leading the Revolution* (Boston: Harvard Business Press, 2002), p. 292.

3   John Hagel and John Seely Brown, *The Only Sustainable Edge: Why Business Strategy Depends on Productive Friction and Dynamic Specialization* (Boston: Harvard Business Press, 2005), pp. 143 – 144.

4   Tony Davila and Daniel Oyon, "Logitech: Passing the Baton to an External CEO" (Stanford, CA: Graduate School of Business, Stanford University, August 2001).

5   Henry Mintzberg, Bruce Ahlstrand, and Joseph Lampel, *Strategy Safari* (New York: Free Press, 2005), p. 34.

6   As of the time of writing, Oracle's acquisition of Sun was still pending approval by European regulators.

7   Pure Digital was acquired by Cisco Systems in 2009.

8   Jefferson Graham, "$29.95 One-Time-Use Video Cameras Ready," *USA Today,* June 5, 2005; retrieved from www.usatoday.com/money/industries /technology/2005-06-05-video-usat_x.htm?csp=34, August 6, 2009.

9   N'Gai Croal, "Gadget of the Stars," *Newsweek,* December 6, 2008.

10 Ryan Kim, "Success in a Flash," *San Francisco Chronicle,* November 30, 2008, p. C-1.

11 Nathan Conz, "Voelker Keeps Progressive on Cutting Edge," *Insurance & Technology,* October 7, 2008; retrieved from www.insurancetech.com /showArticle.jhtml?articleID=210800522, August 8, 2009.

12 Frances X. Frei, "The Four Things a Service Business Must Get Right,"
    Harvard Business Review 86, no. 4 (2008): 74.

Chapter 6   Adaption

1   Toyota and Ford year-end sales reports press releases, December 2006.

2   Jerry Garrett, "Honda Insight: The Once and Future Mileage King," *New York Times,* August 27, 2006.

3   Phillip Vasquez, "Creating Heroes, Championing Change," Design Mind, Issue 05, 2007; retrieved from http://designmind.frogdesign.com/articles/green/creating-heroes-championing-change.html, August 8, 2009.

4   Strictly speaking, there have been four generations of the Prius as of this writing. The very first was launched only in Japan in 1997. What many people think of as the first generation was actually the second, which was launched more widely in 2001. However, the differences between the two were relatively small, and outwardly they were almost identical. For sake of simplicity, what I refer to here as "first generation" is the version first available outside Japan. The fourth generation was launched in the United States in mid-2009.

5   Forest L. Reinhardt, Dennis A. Yao, and Masako Egawa, "Toyota Motor Corporation: Launching Prius," Harvard Business School Case no. 9-706-458 (2006): 10.

6   Ralph Hanson, "Toyota Prius Excels Because of Unique Design," Motor Authority, July 4, 2007; retrieved from www.motorauthority.com/toyota-prius-excels-because-of-unique-design.html, August 6, 2009.

7   Vasquez, "Creating Heroes, Championing Change."

8   John Chris Jones, *Design Methods* (Hoboken, NJ: Wiley, 1992), p. 9.

9   Smith's most recent book covers flexible product development specifically, and has many approaches that are valuable: Preston G. Smith, *Flexible Product Development: Building Agility for Changing Markets* (San Francisco: Jossey-Bass, 2007). Smith collaborated on an earlier book that introduced many of the concepts: Preston G. Smith and Donald G. Reinertsen, *Developing Products in Half the Time* (Hoboken, NJ: Wiley, 1998). Reinertsen dedicates a chapter to the topic of architecture and interfaces in his own book, *Managing the Design Factory: A Product Developer's Toolkit* (New York: Free Press, 1997).

10 Reinertsen, *Managing the Design Factory,* p. 144.

11 Jason Ankeney, "Apple Hints at Looser App Store Rules with iPhone OS 3.0," Fierce Mobile Content, May 5, 2009; retrieved from www.fiercemobilecontent.com/story/apple-hints-looser-app-store-rules-iphone-os-3-0/2009-05-05, August 5, 2009.

12 Smith, *Flexible Product Development,* p. 229.

13 Mitch Wagner, "Twitter Struggles with Downtime, While Fending Off Irked A-List Bloggers," InformationWeek, June 2, 2008; retrieved from www.informationweek.com/blog/main/archives/2008/06/twitter_struggl .html, August 8, 2009.

14 Charles H. Fine, *Clockspeed: Winning Industry Control in the Age of Temporary Advantage* (Reading, MA: Perseus Books, 1998).

15 Baldwin and Clark use an equation to model the reduced value of costly, frequent iterations: $NPV = V - clt$. The NPV of the system is equal to the optimal value of the system minus costs of each iteration (c) x the number of linkages (l) changed each iteration x the number of iterations (t). See Carliss Y. Baldwin and Kim B. Clark, *Design Rules* (Cambridge, MA: MIT Press, 2000).

16 To his credit, Ed Zander, who became CEO of Motorola while the Razr was in development, immediately recognized its potential, and was a supporter for Frost and his team.

17 The Razr's success with women, even before the pink version came out, puts a lie to the stereotype that women only want soft, rounded products. I'm sure that in product team meetings there was concern that its edgy design was too masculine looking, especially in the silver metal finish.

18 Geoffrey Frost, "Motorola's Edge," *Hub,* September 1, 2005; retrieved from www.hubmagazine.com/%3Fp%3D12, August 6, 2009.

19 The Kano model is often used to illustrate this dynamic. Harvard Business School has published a fairly in-depth article about using the Kano model to analyze changing customer preferences and expectations: Marco Iansiti and Ellen Stein, "Understanding User Needs," Harvard Business School Case no. 9-695-051 (1995).

20 Christopher Vollmer says, "Brands today must go beyond simply broadcasting their message; they must beckon the consumer into a conversation. When consumers use digital media to search, shop, blog,

socialize, or seek entertainment, their actions create opportunities for marketers not only to gain insight but also to gather ideas to improve their brands, marketing messages, and media mix choices." And, I would add, the products themselves. Christopher Vollmer, "Digital Darwinism," *Strategy+Business,* no. 54 (Spring 2009): 66.

21   Wade Roush, "The Customer Is Sometimes Wrong," *Technology Review,* October 2005.

22   Malcolm Gladwell nicely documented the story behind the Pepsi Challenge and Coca-Cola's response. See *Blink: The Power of Thinking Without Thinking* (New York: Little, Brown, 2005), pp. 155 – 158.

23   Nicholas Carlson, "Google Misses $200 Million a Year on Image Search," Valleywag, April 24, 2008; retrieved from http://valleywag.gawker.com /383833/google-misses-200-million-a-year-on-image-search, August 5, 2009.

24   Bala Iyer and Thomas H. Davenport, "Reverse Engineering Google's Innovation Machine," *Harvard Business Review* 86, no. 4 (2008): 60.

25   John Battelle, *The Search* (New York: Portfolio, 2005), pp. 93, 123 – 126.

26   Gary Erickson and Lois Ann Lorentzen, *Raising the Bar: Integrity and Passion in Life and Business: A Journey Toward Sustaining Your Business, Brand, People, Community, and the Planet* (San Francisco: Jossey-Bass, 2004), pp. 28 – 32.

27   Adam Richardson, "On Clif Bar and Mountain Climbing," Design Mind, Summer, Issue 04, 2007. Retrieved from http://designmind.frogdesign .com/articles/summer/on-clif-bar-and-mountain-climbing.html, August 7, 2009. For full disclosure, my brother is an employee at Clif Bar.

Chapter 7   Strategy

1   Constantine von Hoffman, "Length of CMO Tenure Continues Decline," Brandweek, August 22, 2006; retrieved from www.brandweek.com /bw/search/article_display.jsp?vnu_content_id=1003020713, August 8, 2009; Robert Weisman, "Being a CEO Has Its Perks, but Tenure Isn't One of Them," *Boston Globe,* May 11, 2008; retrieved from www.boston.com /business/articles/2008/05/11/being_a_ceo_has_its_perks_but_tenure_ isnt_one_of_them/, August 8, 2009.

2   Preston G. Smith and Donald G. Reinertsen, *Developing Products in Half the Time* (Hoboken, NJ: Wiley, 1998), p. 3.

3   Gary Hamel, *Leading the Revolution* (Boston: Harvard Business Press, 2002), pp. 275 – 276.

4   Adam Richardson, "On Clif Bar and Mountain Climbing," Design Mind, Summer, Issue 04, 2007. Retrieved from http://designmind.frogdesign .com/articles/summer/on-clif-bar-and-mountain-climbing.html, August 7, 2009.

5   William McDonaugh and Michael Brangart, *Cradle to Cradle* (New York: Farrar, Straus & Giroux, 2002).

6   John Battelle, *The Search* (New York: Portfolio, 2005), p. 141.

7   Paul McNamara, "Almost Half of Google Products—Including 4-Year-Old Gmail—Remain in Beta: Why?" NetworkWorld Buzzblog, September 24, 2008. Retrieved from www.networkworld.com/community /node/33131, August 7, 2009.

8   Charles Fishman, "This Is a Marketing Revolution," *Fast Company*, December 19, 2007; retrieved from www.fastcompany.com/magazine /24/capone.html, August 5, 2009.

9   Michael Schrage, *Serious Play: How the World's Best Companies Simulate to Innovate* (Boston: Harvard Business Press, 2000), p. 47.

10   See the Dyson Web site, www.dyson.com/about/story. There are actually conflicting figures around the duration of time spent developing the first Dyson vacuum cleaner, even on Dyson's own Web site. Some places five years is given, sometimes fifteen. This variance is found in many articles about and interviews with Dyson also. Whether it is purposeful mystique-building or just a simple case of mismanagement of the foundation myth, I don't know.

11   Schrage, *Serious Play*, p. 20.

12   Schrage, *Serious Play*, p. 20.

13   Schrage, *Serious Play*, p. 29.

14   Vindu Goel, "How Google Decides to Pull the Plug," *New York Times*, February 15, 2009.

15   For example, see Henry W. Chesbrough, *Open Innovation* (Boston: Harvard Business Press, 2003); Henry W. Chesbrough and Melissa

Appleyard, "Open Innovation and Strategy," *California Management Review* 50, no. 1 (2007); Larry Huston and Nabil Sakkab, "Connect and Develop: Inside Procter & Gamble's New Model for Innovation," *Harvard Business Review* 84, no. 3 (2006); Ron Adner, "Match Your Innovation Strategy to Your Innovation Ecosystem," *Harvard Business Review* 84, no. 4 (2006); Gary P. Pisano and Roberto Verganti, "Which Kind of Collaboration Is Right for You?" *Harvard Business Review* 86, no. 12 (2008): 78 – 86.

16 William Buxton, *Sketching User Experiences: Getting the Design Right and the Right Design* (San Francisco: Morgan Kaufmann, 2007), pp. 70 – 71.

17 Marco Iansiti and Roy Levien, *The Keystone Advantage: What the New Dynamics of Business Ecosystems Mean for Strategy, Innovation, and Sustainability* (Boston: Harvard Business Press, 2004), pp. 61 – 62, 76.

18 Clayton M. Christensen and Michael E. Raynor, *The Innovator's Solution: Creating and Sustaining Successful Growth* (Boston: Harvard Business Press, 2003), pp. 125 – 142; Geoffrey A. Moore, *Dealing with Darwin: How Great Companies Innovate at Every Phase of Their Evolution* (New York: Portfolio, 2006), pp. 29 – 55.

19 The iPhone's reception, call, and camera quality, for example, were not that great compared to some other smartphones, and the iPod had less storage capacity than much cheaper players when it debuted.

20 iTunes was based on the older SoundJam application, which Apple bought and updated. The scroll-wheel of the iPod is essentially just a circular trackpad like that found on laptops, and was licensed from Synaptics. The iPod OS was a combination of elements from Portal Player and Pixo. The Fairplay digital rights management technology used in the music store was invented by Veridisc.

21 Vidya L. Drego, "Best Practices in the Out-of-Box Experience" (Cambridge, MA: Forrester, April 2008).

Chapter 8   Organization

1   E. Jeffrey Conklin, *Dialogue Mapping: Building Shared Understanding of Wicked Problems* (Hoboken, NJ: Wiley, 2006), pp. 34 – 38.

2 Ben R. Rich, *Skunk Works* (New York: Little, Brown, 1996), pp. 19 – 21.

3 Grant McCracken, *Flock and Flow: Predicting and Managing Change in a Dynamic Marketplace* (Bloomington: Indiana University Press, 2006), p. 133.

4 Gary Erickson and Lois Ann Lorentzen, *Raising the Bar: Integrity and Passion in Life and Business: A Journey Toward Sustaining Your Business, Brand, People, Community, and the Planet* (San Francisco: Jossey-Bass, 2004), p. 256.

5 Mark Hurst, "Interview: Maryam Mohit, Amazon.com," November 21, 2002; retrieved from www.goodexperience.com/blog/archives/000192 .php, August 6, 2009.

6 Saul Hansell, "Curious at Amazon, but Not Idle," *New York Times,* March 27, 2009; retrieved from http://bits.blogs.nytimes.com/2009/03/27 /curious-at-amazon-but-not-idle/, August 6, 2009.

7 McCracken, *Flock and Flow,* pp. 133 – 134.

8 Bruce Temkin, Interview with author, March 10, 2009.

9 Kevin C. Desouza, *Managing Knowledge with Artificial Intelligence: An Introduction with Guidelines for Nonspecialists* (Westport, CT: Quorum Books, 2002), p. 17.

10 John Hagel and John Seely Brown, *The Only Sustainable Edge: Why Business Strategy Depends on Productive Friction and Dynamic Specialization* (Boston: Harvard Business Press, 2005), p. 100.

11 Ed Catmull, "How Pixar Fosters Collective Creativity," *Harvard Business Review* 86, no. 9 (2008): 70 – 71.

12 Preston Smith writes about various location models, discussing their pros and cons, in *Flexible Product Development: Building Agility for Changing Markets* (San Francisco: Jossey-Bass, 2007), pp. 141 – 152. He also discusses how co-location practices are built into agile programming for software. He and Reinertsen discuss co-location in an earlier book: Preston G. Smith and Donald G. Reinertsen, *Developing Products in Half the Time* (Hoboken, NJ: Wiley, 1998).

13 Jonathan Copulsky and Ken Hutt, "Gambling with the House's Money: The Randomness of Corporate Innovation" (Chicago: Deloitte, 2006).

14 Copulsky and Hutt, "Gambling with the House's Money."

15 Rosabeth Moss Kanter, "Innovation: The Classic Traps," *Harvard Business Review,* 84, no. 11 (2006).

16 Bala Iyer and Thomas H. Davenport note that, regrettably, nontechnical and nonmanagerial employees are not given the same innovation incentives or time allocations. Who knows what ideas these "non-experts" could come up with, either for actual Google products or for innovations on internal processes and practices? See Bala Iyer and Thomas H. Davenport, "Reverse Engineering Google's Innovation Machine," *Harvard Business Review* 86, no. 4 (2008): 64.

17 Henry W. Chesbrough, *Open Innovation* (Boston: Harvard Business Press, 2003), pp. xviii – xix.

18 The four examples noted here were covered on Public Radio International's business program, *Marketplace,* interviewing Bill Carter: "Desperate Networks." Available online at http://marketplace.publicradio .org/shows/2006/05/02/PM200605025.html. See also Bill Carter's book, *Desperate Networks* (New York: Broadway Books, 2006).

19 Richard Buchanan used the term *placements* to describe a similar concept in his own thinking on wicked problems. He says, "Placements are the tools by which a designer intuitively or deliberately shapes a design situation, identifying the views of all participants, the issues which concern them, and the invention that will serve as a working hypothesis for exploration and development." I find *placements* too abstract a term, however, and have found people get the concept of pattern experience readily. See Victor Margolin and Richard Buchanan, *The Idea of Design* (Cambridge, MA: MIT Press, 1995), pp. 3 – 20.

20 Henry Mintzberg, Bruce Ahlstrand, and Joseph Lampel, *Strategy Safari* (New York: Free Press, 2005), pp. 195 – 198.

21 Chip Heath and Dan Heath, *Made to Stick: Why Some Ideas Survive and Others Die* (New York: Random House, 2007), p. 18.

22 Adam Richardson, "On Clif Bar and Mountain Climbing," Design Mind, Summer, Issue 04, 2007. Retrieved from http://designmind.frogdesign .com/articles/summer/on-clif-bar-and-mountain-climbing.html, August 7, 2009.

Chapter 9   Truths

1 Brian Hindo, "At 3M, a Struggle Between Efficiency and Creativity," *Business Week,* June 11, 2007.

2 Ed Catmull, "How Pixar Fosters Collective Creativity," *Harvard Business Review* 86, no. 9 (2008): 66.

Bibliography

Adner, Ron. "Match Your Innovation Strategy to Your Innovation Ecosystem." *Harvard Business Review*, 2006, *84*(4), 98 – 107.

Ankeney, Jason. "Apple Hints at Looser App Store Rules with iPhone OS 3.0." Fierce Mobile Content, May 5, 2009. Retrieved from www.fiercemobile content.com/story/apple-hints-looser-app-store-rules-iphone-os-3-0/2009 -05-05, August 5, 2009.

Baldwin, Carliss Y., and Kim B. Clark. *Design Rules*. Cambridge, MA: MIT Press, 2000.

Battelle, John. *The Search*. New York: Portfolio, 2005.

Bergman, Eric. *Information Appliances and Beyond: Interaction Design for Consumer Products*. San Francisco: Morgan Kaufmann, 2000.

Beyer, Hugh, and Karen Holtzblatt. *Contextual Design: Defining Customer-Centered Systems*. San Francisco: Morgan Kaufmann, 1998.

Brown, John Seely, and Paul Duguid. *The Social Life of Information*. Boston: Harvard Business Press, 2002.

Buxton, William. *Sketching User Experiences: Getting the Design Right and the Right Design*. San Francisco: Morgan Kaufmann, 2007.

Camillus, J. C. "Strategy as a Wicked Problem." *Harvard Business Review*, 2008, *86*(5), 98.

Carlson, Nicholas. "Google Misses $200 Million a Year on Image Search." Valleywag, April 24, 2008. Retrieved from http://valleywag.gawker.com/383833/google-misses-200-million-a-year-on-image-search, August 5, 2009.

Carter, Bill. *Desperate Networks.* New York: Broadway Books, 2006.

Catmull, Ed. "How Pixar Fosters Collective Creativity." *Harvard Business Review*, 2008, *86*(9), 64 – 72.

Cha, Arian Eunjung. "In Retail, Profiling for Profit." *Washington Post*, August 17, 2005.

Chesbrough, Henry W. *Open Innovation.* Boston: Harvard Business Press, 2003.

Chesbrough, Henry, and Melissa Appleyard. "Open Innovation and Strategy." *California Management Review*, 2007, *50*(1).

Christensen, Clayton M. *The Innovator's Dilemma: When New Technologies Cause Great Firms to Fail.* Boston: Harvard Business Press, 1997.

Christensen, Clayton M., and Michael E. Raynor. *The Innovator's Solution: Creating and Sustaining Successful Growth.* Boston: Harvard Business Press, 2003.

Christensen, Clayton M., Scott D. Anthony, Gerald Berstell, and Denise Nitterhouse. "Finding the Right Job for Your Product." *MIT Sloan Management Review*, Spring 2007, pp. 2 – 10.

Conklin, E. Jeffrey. *Dialogue Mapping: Building Shared Understanding of Wicked Problems.* Hoboken, NJ: Wiley, 2006.

Conz, Nathan. "Voelker Keeps Progressive on Cutting Edge." Insurance & Technology, October 7, 2008. Retrieved from www.insurancetech.com/showArticle.jhtml?articleID=210800522, August 8, 2009.

Copulsky, Jonathan, and Ken Hutt. "Gambling with the House's Money: The Randomness of Corporate Innovation." Chicago: Deloitte, 2006.

Croal, N'Gai. "Gadget of the Stars." *Newsweek*, December 6, 2008.

Csikszentmihalyi, Mihaly. *Flow: The Psychology of Optimal Experience.* New York: HarperPerennial, 1991.

Davila, Tony, and Daniel Oyon. "Logitech: Passing the Baton to an External CEO." Case study. Stanford, CA: Graduate School of Business, Stanford University, August 2001.

Davila, Tony, Marc J. Epstein, and Robert D. Shelton. *Making Innovation Work: How to Manage It, Measure It, and Profit from It.* Upper Saddle River, NJ: Wharton School, 2006.

Day, George S., and Paul J. H. Schoemaker. *Peripheral Vision: Detecting the Weak Signals That Will Make or Break Your Company.* Boston: Harvard Business Press, 2006.

"Dazzled by Digits: How We're Wooed by Product Specifications." Research Digest Blog, November 14, 2008. Retrieved from http://bps-research-digest .blogspot.com/2008/11/dazzled-by-digits-how-were-wooed-by.html, August 5, 2009.

Desouza, Kevin C. *Managing Knowledge with Artificial Intelligence: An Introduction with Guidelines for Nonspecialists.* Westport, CT: Quorum Books, 2002.

"Desperate Networks." *Marketplace*, May 2, 2006. Retrieved from http:// marketplace.publicradio.org/shows/2006/05/02/PM200605025.html, August 5, 2009.

Deutschman, Alan. *The Second Coming of Steve Jobs.* New York: Broadway Books, 2000.

Drego, Vidya L. "Best Practices in the Out-of-Box Experience." Cambridge, MA: Forrester, April 2008.

Economist Intelligence Unit. "The Innovators: How Successful Companies Drive Business Transformation." *The Economist* (September 2008).

Erickson, Gary, and Lois Ann Lorentzen. *Raising the Bar: Integrity and Passion in Life and Business: A Journey Toward Sustaining Your Business, Brand, People, Community, and the Planet.* San Francisco: Jossey-Bass, 2004.

Fine, Charles H. *Clockspeed: Winning Industry Control in the Age of Temporary Advantage.* Reading, MA: Perseus Books, 1998.

Fiorina, Carly. *Tough Choices.* New York: Penguin, 2006.

Fishman, Charles. "This Is a Marketing Revolution." *Fast Company*, December 19, 2007. Retrieved from www.fastcompany.com/magazine/24/capone.html, August 5, 2009.

Frei, Frances X. "The Four Things a Service Business Must Get Right." *Harvard Business Review*, 2008, 86(4), 70 – 78.

"Friends of Buick FAQ." Retrieved from www.friendsofbuick.com/about.html, August 5, 2009.

Frost, Geoffrey. "Motorola's Edge." *The Hub*, September 1, 2005. Retrieved from www.hubmagazine.com/%3Fp%3D12, August 6, 2009.

"Fuck Everything, We're Doing Five Blades." *The Onion*, February 18, 2004. Retrieved from www.theonion.com/content/node/33930, August 7, 2009.

Gaither, Chris. "Google Puts Lid on New Products; Realizing That Its Myriad Services Are Confusing Users, It Will Focus on Refining What It Has." *Los Angeles Times*, October 6, 2006.

Garrett, Jerry. "Honda Insight: The Once and Future Mileage King." *New York Times*, August 27, 2006.

"Gillette Unveils 5-Bladed Razor." CNN Money, September 14, 2005. Retrieved from http://money.cnn.com/2005/09/14/news/fortune500/gillette/, August 5, 2009.

Gladwell, Malcolm. *Blink: The Power of Thinking Without Thinking*. New York: Little, Brown, 2005.

"Global CEO Study, 2008: The Enterprise of the Future." IBM, May 2008. Retrieved from http://ibm.com/ibm/ideasfromibm/us/ceo/20080505/, September 16, 2009.

Goel, Vindu. "How Google Decides to Pull the Plug." *New York Times*, February 15, 2009.

Goldstein, Daniel J., Eric J. Johnson, Andreas Herrmann, and Mark Heitmann. "Nudge Your Customers Toward Better Choices." *Harvard Business Review*, 2008, *86*(12), 99 – 105.

Goodwin, Kim. *Designing for the Digital Age: How to Create Human-Centered Products and Services*. Hoboken, NJ: Wiley, 2009.

Gould, Stephen Jay. *Full House*. New York: Three Rivers Press, 1996.

Graham, Jefferson. "$29.95 One-Time-Use Video Cameras Ready." *USA Today*, June 5, 2005. Retrieved from www.usatoday.com/money/industries /technology/2005-06-05-video-usat_x.htm?csp=34, August 6, 2009.

Hagel, John, and John Seely Brown. *The Only Sustainable Edge: Why Business Strategy Depends on Productive Friction and Dynamic Specialization*. Boston: Harvard Business Press, 2005.

Hamel, Gary. "Killer Strategies That Make Shareholders Rich." *Fortune Magazine*, June 1997, pp. 76 – 77.

Hamel, Gary. *Leading the Revolution*. Boston: Harvard Business Press, 2002.

Hamel, Gary, and C. K. Prahalad. "The Core Competence of the Corporation." *Harvard Business Review*, 1990, *68*(3), 79 – 91.

Hansell, Saul. "Curious at Amazon, but Not Idle." *New York Times*, March 27, 2009. Retrieved from http://bits.blogs.nytimes.com/2009/03/27/curious-at-amazon-but-not-idle/, August 6, 2009.

Hanson, Ralph. "Toyota Prius Excels Because of Unique Design." Motor Authority, July 4, 2007. Retrieved from www.motorauthority.com/toyota-prius-excels-because-of-unique-design.html, August 6, 2009.

Hart, Myra, Michael Roberts, and Julia Stevens. "Zipcar: Refining the Business Model." Harvard Business School Case no. 9-803-09, 2005.

Heath, Chip, and Dan Heath. *Made to Stick: Why Some Ideas Survive and Others Die.* New York: Random House, 2007.

Hindo, Brian. "At 3M, A Struggle Between Efficiency and Creativity." June 11, 2007. Retrieved from www.businessweek.com/magazine/content/07_24/b4038406.htm, September 13, 2009.

Hurst, Mark. "Interview: Maryam Mohit, Amazon.com." November 21, 2002. Retrieved from www.goodexperience.com/blog/archives/000192.php, August 6, 2009.

Huston, Larry, and Nabil Sakkab. "Connect and Develop: Inside Procter & Gamble's New Model for Innovation." *Harvard Business Review*, 2006, *84*(3).

Iansiti, Marco, and Ellen Stein. "Understanding User Needs." Harvard Business School Case no. 9-695-051 (1995).

Iansiti, Marco, and Roy Levien. *The Keystone Advantage: What the New Dynamics of Business Ecosystems Mean for Strategy, Innovation, and Sustainability.* Boston: Harvard Business Press, 2004.

Imhoff, Daniel. *Paper or Plastic: Searching for Solutions for an Overpackaged World.* San Francisco: Sierra Club Books, 2005.

Iyer, Bala, and Thomas H. Davenport. "Reverse Engineering Google's Innovation Machine." *Harvard Business Review*, 2008, *86*(4), 58 – 68.

Jana, Reena. "How to Build a 60-mph Oven." *Business Week*, July 6, 2006. Retrieved from www.businessweek.com/innovate/content/jul2006/id20060706_182903.htm, August 7, 2009.

Jones, John Chris. *Design Methods.* Hoboken, NJ: Wiley, 1992.

Kanter, Rosabeth Moss. "Innovation: The Classic Traps." *Harvard Business Review*, 2006, *84*(11), 72 – 83.

Kemper, Steve. *Code Name Ginger: The Story Behind Segway and Dean Kamen's Quest to Invent a New World.* Boston: Harvard Business Press, 2003.

Kim, Ryan. "Success in a Flash." *San Francisco Chronicle*, November 30, 2008, p. C-1.

Kim, W. Chan, and Renée Mauborgne. *Blue Ocean Strategy: How to Create Uncontested Market Space and Make the Competition Irrelevant.* Boston: Harvard Business Press, 2005.

Kuniavsky, Mike. *Observing the User Experience.* San Francisco: Morgan Kaufmann, 2003.

Laurel, Brenda. *Design Research: Methods and Perspectives.* Cambridge, MA: MIT Press, 2003.

Luckey, David S., and Kevin P. Schultz. "Defining and Coping with Wicked Problems: The Case of Fort Ord Building Removal." Monterey, CA: Naval Post-Graduate School, March, 2001.

Margolin, Victor, and Richard Buchanan. *The Idea of Design.* Cambridge, MA: MIT Press, 1995.

McCarthy, Ryan, Nadine Heintz, and Bo Burlingham. "Starting Up in a Down Economy." *Inc*, May 2006.

McCracken, Grant. *Flock and Flow: Predicting and Managing Change in a Dynamic Marketplace.* Bloomington: Indiana University Press, 2006.

McCracken, Grant. "Innovations for the Innovator." This Blog Sits at the Intersection of Anthropology and Economics, October 24, 2006. Retrieved from www.cultureby.com/trilogy/2006/10/innovators_inno.html, August 7, 2009.

McDonough, William, and Michael Brangart. *Cradle to Cradle.* New York: Farrar, Straus & Giroux, 2002.

McGrath, Michael E. *Product Strategy for High Technology Companies: Accelerating Your Business to Web Speed.* New York: McGraw-Hill, 2001.

McNamara, Paul. "Almost Half of Google Products—Including 4-Year-Old Gmail—Remain in Beta: Why?" NetworkWorld Buzzblog, September 24, 2008. Retrieved from www.networkworld.com/community/node/33131, August 7, 2009.

McPhee, John. *The John McPhee Reader.* New York: Farrar, Straus & Giroux, 1982.

Merholz, Peter. "Peter Talks Shop with Zipcar CEO Scott Griffith." Adaptive Path, January 23, 2008. Retrieved from www.adaptivepath.com/ideas/essays/archives/000896.php, August 7, 2009.

Miller, Paul. "Verizon Passed Up Apple iPhone Deal." Engadget Mobile, January 29, 2007. Retrieved from www.engadgetmobile.com/2007/01/29/verizon-passed-up-apple-iphone-deal/, August 7, 2009.

Mintzberg, Henry, Bruce Ahlstrand, and Joseph Lampel. *Strategy Safari.* New York: Free Press, 2005.

Moon, Youngme. "Break Free from the Product Life Cycle." *Harvard Business Review*, 2005, *83*(5), 86 – 94.

Moore, Geoffrey A. *Dealing with Darwin: How Great Companies Innovate at Every Phase of Their Evolution.* New York: Portfolio, 2006.

Neumeier, Marty. *The Designful Company.* Berkeley, CA: Peachpit Press, 2008.

Pascale, Richard T. "The Honda Effect Revisited." *California Management Review*, 1996, *38*(4).

Penguin Books. "About Penguin: Company History." Penguin UK Web site, n.d. Retrieved from www.penguin.co.uk/static/packages/uk/aboutus/history.html, August 7, 2009.

Pine, B. Joseph, and James H. Gilmore. *The Experience Economy: Work Is Theatre & Every Business a Stage.* Boston: Harvard Business Press, 1999.

Pink, Daniel H. *A Whole New Mind: Moving from the Information Age to the Conceptual Age.* New York: Riverhead Books, 2005.

Pisano, Gary P., and Roberto Verganti. "Which Kind of Collaboration Is Right for You?" *Harvard Business Review*, 2008, *86*(12), 78 – 86.

Reinertsen, Donald G. *Managing the Design Factory: A Product Developer's Toolkit.* New York: Free Press, 1997.

Reinhardt, Forest L., Dennis A. Yao, and Masako Egawa. "Toyota Motor Corporation: Launching Prius." Harvard Business School Case no. 9-706-458 Case (2006).

Rich, Ben R. *Skunk Works.* New York: Little, Brown, 1996.

Richardson, Adam. "On Clif Bar and Mountain Climbing." Design Mind, Summer, Issue 04, 2007. Retrieved from http://designmind.frogdesign.com/articles/summer/on-clif-bar-and-mountain-climbing.html, August 7, 2009.

Rittel, H.W.J. "On the Planning Crisis: Systems Analysis of 'The First and Second Generations.'" *Bedriftsokonomen*, 1972, no. 8.

Roberts, Nancy. "Coping with Wicked Problems: The Case of Afghanistan." *Learning from International Public Management Reform*, 2001, 11B, 353 – 355.

Rosen, Emanuel. *The Anatomy of Buzz: How to Create Word-of-Mouth Marketing.* New York: Doubleday Business, 2002.

Roush, Wade. "The Customer Is Sometimes Wrong." *Technology Review*, October 2005.

Schrage, Michael. *Serious Play: How the World's Best Companies Simulate to Innovate.* Boston: Harvard Business Press, 2000.

Schwartz, Barry. *The Paradox of Choice: Why More Is Less.* New York: Ecco, 2004.

Smith, Preston G. *Flexible Product Development: Building Agility for Changing Markets.* San Francisco: Jossey-Bass, 2007.

Smith, Preston G., and Donald G. Reinertsen. *Developing Products in Half the Time.* Hoboken, NJ: Wiley, 1998.

Surowiecki, James. "Feature Presentation." *New Yorker*, May 28, 2007.

Temkin, Bruce. "Brands Are Dying; Deal with It." Forrester, March 6, 2009. Retrieved from http://experiencematters.wordpress.com/2009/03/06/brands-are-dying-deal-with-it/, August 8, 2009.

Temkin, Bruce D. "Customer Experience Correlates to Loyalty." Cambridge, MA: Forrester, February 17, 2009.

Thaler, Richard H., and Cass R. Sunstein. *Nudge: Improving Decisions About Health, Wealth, and Happiness.* New Haven, CT: Yale University Press, 2008.

Trott, Paul. *Innovation Management and New Product Development.* Essex, England: Pearson Education, 2008.

Ulwick, Anthony. "Turn Customer Input into Innovation." *Harvard Business Review*, 2002, *80*(1), 91–98.

Ulwick, Anthony. *What Customers Want.* New York: McGraw-Hill, 2005.

Vasquez, Phillip. "Creating Heroes, Championing Change." Design Mind, Green, Issue 05, 2007. Retrieved from http://designmind.frogdesign.com/articles/green/creating-heroes-championing-change.html, August 8, 2009.

Vollmer, Christopher. "Digital Darwinism." *Strategy+Business*, Spring 2009, no. 54, pp. 58–69.

von Hippel, Eric. *Democratizing Innovation.* Cambridge, MA: MIT Press, 2005.

von Hippel, Eric. "Lead Users: A Source of Novel Product Concepts." *Management Science*, 1986, 32(7), 791–805.

von Hippel, Eric, Stefan Thomke, and Mary Sonnack. "Creating Breakthroughs at 3M." *Harvard Business Review*, 1999, 77(5).

von Hoffman, Constantine. "Length of CMO Tenure Continues Decline." Brandweek, August 22, 2006. Retrieved from www.brandweek.com/bw /search/article_display.jsp?vnu_content_id=1003020713, August 8, 2009.

Wagner, Mitch. "Twitter Struggles with Downtime, While Fending Off Irked A-List Bloggers." InformationWeek, June 2, 2008. Retrieved from www .informationweek.com/blog/main/archives/2008/06/twitter_struggl.html, August 8, 2009.

Walton, Mary. *Car.* New York: Norton, 1999.

"Water Filtration in the United States, 2008." Dublin, Ireland: Research and Markets, 2008.

Weisman, Robert. "Being a CEO Has Its Perks, but Tenure Isn't One of Them." *Boston Globe*, May 11, 2008. Retrieved from www.boston.com /business/articles/2008/05/11/being_a_ceo_has_its_perks_but_tenure_isnt _one_of_them/, August 8, 2009.

Zaltman, Gerald. *How Customers Think.* Boston: Harvard Business Press, 2003.

Acknowledgments

There are many places I could start when acknowledging those who have helped me chart the circuitous course resulting in the thinking and experience contained in these pages. I could begin with the chance encounter I had as a teenager with a car designer while walking in the Lake District in northern England, who showed me that there actually is a profession of design, giving me a path from my boyhood drawings to a future career. I could recall Ed Hill, my late art teacher from high school in California, who gave me the latitude and, for the first time, the right tools to do the kind of design I wanted to.

I could go back to Victor Margolin and Larry Solomon, who took a chance on a twenty-three-year-old and published my first-ever article in their journal *Design Issues*. Or to Gerald Graff, the founder of the multidisciplinary master's program at the University of Chicago that allowed me to shift course from designer to user researcher and strategist.

All these events, big and small, played a role. The same can be said for all the projects I have worked on over the years, for dozens of clients; in one way or another they have all contributed to the ideas laid out here by presenting challenging problems that required new thinking and approaches. I owe a lot to all the staff at frog design that I work alongside, who have brought their own diverse perspectives and amazing talents to these challenges, and from whom I continue to learn every day.

I am greatly appreciative of all the people who provided input and perspectives and additional ideas on the early drafts, especially Gianluca Brugnoli, Ivan Croxford, John Goyert, Jon Kolko, Brooks Protzmann, Laura Richardson (no relation), Steve Sato, Adam Silver, and Clay Wiedemann. I also want to thank Bill O'Connor of Autodesk, who was instrumental in securing several interviews with people quoted in the book, and has been in general an enthusiastic supporter. Thanks to Remy Labesque for lending his talents to the product illustrations in the book.

I am indebted to the frog design executive team, in particular Doreen Lorenzo, Tim Leberecht, Kate Swann, Mark Rolston, and Aimee Jungmann, for taking the leap of faith in giving me the time to work on the book, and providing great support throughout its conception and launch.

Thanks to my editor, Karen Murphy, for her enthusiasm and energy.

And thanks finally to my wife, Leslie, for her unending support, her help with the diagrams used in these pages, and her patience in putting up with my absent-mindedness while I was preoccupied with writing.

About the Author

Adam Richardson is a creative director at frog design, inc., a global innovation and design consultancy, where he has worked with organizations such as HP, Microsoft, Chrysler, NASA, Vodafone, LG, Humana, and Nike. His background combines experience in product development, interaction design, product strategy, and customer research. He earned his BFA in Industrial Design from the California College of the Arts, and earned a multi-disciplinary MA from the University of Chicago in 1997. He writes regularly on design and business and speaks at conferences worldwide. In addition to having taught design and user research, he is a guest lecturer at the École Nationale Supérieure de Création Industrielle in Paris, and at the IESE University of Navarra in Barcelona.

Index